point of grace
girls of grace
devotional and Bible study workbook

Make It Real

point of grace

girls of grace

devotional and Bible study workbook

Make It Real

words, worth, relationships, and me

OUR PURPOSE AT HOWARD PUBLISHING IS TO:

- *Increase faith* in the hearts of growing Christians
- *Inspire holiness* in the lives of believers
- *Instill hope* in the hearts of struggling people everywhere

BECAUSE HE'S COMING AGAIN!

Published by Howard Publishing Co., Inc.
3117 North Seventh Street, West Monroe, Louisiana 71291-2227

Study guides by Whitney Prosperi
Edited by Philis Boultinghouse
Interior design by John Mark Luke Designs
Cover design by LinDee Loveland
Cover photo by Aaron Rapoport

ISBN 1-58229-462-3

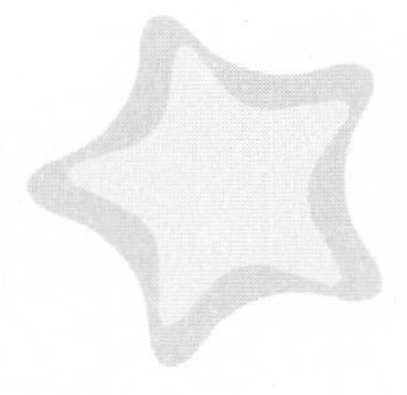

We would like to dedicate this book to all the Girls of Grace conference attendees, past and future. You continue to encourage us by your desire to walk in a manner worthy of our Lord Jesus Christ.

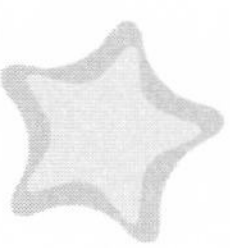

Contents

A friend loves at all times,
and a brother is born for adversity.
Proverbs 17:17

Introduction

It is with great joy that we introduce our new devotional and Bible study to you. We are so passionate about the content, and we are hopeful that you will find lots of relevant information to help you at school and at home. After leading the Girls of Grace conferences for the past three years, we are even more inspired by your lives and testimonies. We understand so much more now just how hard it is to live where you live, to be a teenage girl in our culture. We pray often for all of you—that your convictions will be strong and able to withstand the pressure of all that is coming toward you. It is also our prayer that God will keep you in His care and protect you always. Girls, don't ever forget who you are in Christ and that with the power of the Holy Spirit living in you, you truly can do all things through Christ who strengthens you.

In this book we have really tried to "make it real" for you. We have shared our hearts on a variety of topics, including gossip, self-esteem, mentors, and more. Just as you've shared your hearts with us through the years, we hope to inspire you by sharing ours. We want you to know us better when you complete this devotional and Bible study, and we think that you will. But more than that, it is our prayer that you would know our precious Lord better, and that He will continue to shape and mold you to be more like Him.

All our love,

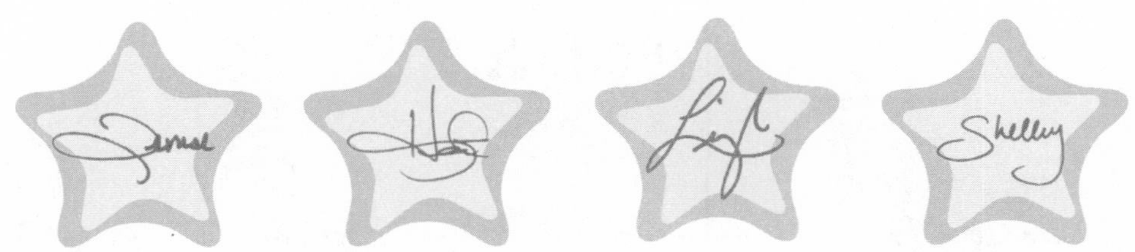

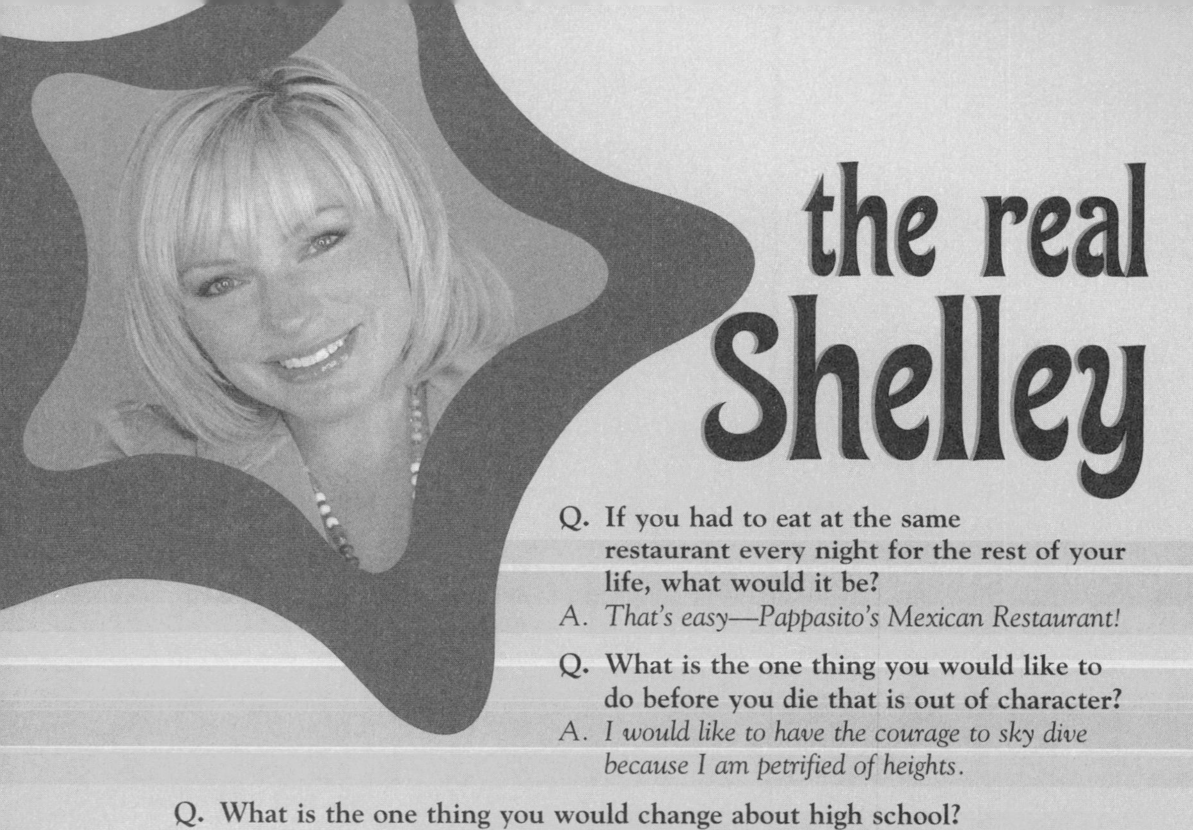

the real Shelley

Q. If you had to eat at the same restaurant every night for the rest of your life, what would it be?
A. *That's easy—Pappasito's Mexican Restaurant!*

Q. What is the one thing you would like to do before you die that is out of character?
A. *I would like to have the courage to sky dive because I am petrified of heights.*

Q. What is the one thing you would change about high school?
A. *I would put myself on the homecoming court (preferably as queen).*

Q. What is the one material possession you would take from Heather?
A. *Her collection of tea cups.*

Q. What characteristic do you love most about yourself?
A. *I have pretty good organizational skills.*

Q. What is the most embarrassing thing about yourself?
A. *I have to wear a girdle almost every day to hold my stomach in . . . I affectionately call it the "torture suit."*

Q. What is the one thing you tried out for and never made?
A. *I tried out for the singing group Truth (several times) and never made it.*

the gift of gab

If we can control our tongues,
we'll have the discipline to control
ourselves in every other way.

The LORD *. . . delights in pure words.*
Proverbs 15:26 NLT

Mighty Mouth

We've all done it, haven't we?

You know how it works: our mind formulates some negative or rude comment that makes its way to our tongue faster than a speeding bullet, and *bam!*—out it comes, wounding whoever is in its path. The book of Proverbs says, "Reckless words pierce like a sword" (12:18). Now, I've never actually been pierced by a sword, but something tells me it would really hurt!

Have you ever been really hurt? I don't mean physically, like by a sword or from a broken arm; I mean emotionally raked over the coals. Have the words of someone ever cut to the quick of your soul and made your feelings cry out, "Ouch!"? Let me pose another question to you: have you ever really hurt someone else? Have you said something that wounded another person deeply, something you wished so badly you could take back, but the bullet had already been fired?

If I were to respond to these questions honestly, the answer would be absolutely yes to both. I've dished it out, and I've taken it. Unfortunately, I've done a little more dishing than taking, and I'm just guessing, but something tells me that many of you have too.

For some reason we females are abundantly blessed with the gift of gab. And we don't always use that gift for good. Now, not all girls are big talkers. I know some beautiful girls who are shy, meek, and absolutely precious—but that is not how I would describe myself. (Well, maybe the "precious" part!) Seriously though, most girls were just plain born to talk. We're born to yak—about everything! All the time! Without ceasing! I remember in junior high school I thought the verse "Pray without ceasing" said "Talk without ceasing," 'cause that's what I did—all the time. I kid you not.

I would get my grades every quarter, and I would get straight As, almost always. But the conduct grades were another story. There were basically three behavior levels: U was for "unsatisfactory behavior." That was for the boys who did awful stuff like skip class, curse at the teacher—you know the ones. Then there was N for "needs improvement." And of course S stood for "satisfactory," which was achieved by all the kids who didn't suffer from loose lips like I did. Even though I was pretty book smart, I got straight Ns all the time. My parents would get so mad. Straight As and straight Ns. If I was so smart, how come I needed improvement? I was somewhat of a perfectionist, so I really wanted As and Ss, but if I'd ever gotten any Ss, they would have stood for "shut up"!

Oh well, I suppose all of us girls need a little improvement when it comes to using our mouths the way God intended.

Words That Hurt, Words That Heal

One of the guys in our band used to say, "Words that hurt, words that heal" to remind us to watch our mouths whenever the conversation turned gossipy. Our words have mighty power—for good or for bad. And we can't use the excuse that we just "can't help" what we say. For through the power of the Holy Spirit living in us, we really do have the ability to choose how we use our words. As girls striving to become more Christlike, we can actually choose to use our words to help and heal others, instead of to hurt them. Just because we're girls and come by our talking honestly doesn't mean we have free rein to say what we feel.

Our tongues can turn us into hypocrites before we know it: "If you claim to be religious but don't control your tongue, you are just fooling yourself, and your religion is worthless" (James 1:26 NLT). These are pretty strong words. James is telling us that even if we are religious in other areas of our lives, if we can't control what we say, our religion is *worthless*. That's an awful lot of emphasis on our speech. But if we can control our tongues, we'll have the discipline to control ourselves in every other way. According to James, the tongue is harder to control, or tame, than any wild creature in the world (3:7–8). He doesn't say this to discourage us from trying to control our tongues but to remind us to be very serious in our watch over our mighty mouth.

The book of Proverbs speaks strongly about our tongues too. It says we are "wicked" when we speak corrupt words: "The godly speak words that are helpful, but the wicked speak only what is corrupt" (Proverbs 10:32 NLT). That seems pretty harsh, but when we consider what is going on in our society today, especially among teenage girls, the description actually is very fitting.

Mean Girls

Some of you, no doubt, have seen the movie *Mean Girls*, starring Lindsay Lohan. Now I'm not supporting the values displayed in this particular flick; but the movie was very enlightening, because it exposes all the ugly things that really happen in our high schools today. It used to be that the word *bully* was associated only with boys, but now bullying is rampant among teenage girls. That is, pushing people around, whether physically or otherwise, just to make yourself feel like a bigger person. Bullying is downright *mean*!

In the movie Caddie (pronounced "Katie"), played by Lohan, is the new girl at school. Having been homeschooled her whole life, Caddie desperately wants to be accepted at her new high school. She quickly becomes friends with Regina George, the beauty queen who is the self-proclaimed leader of the most popular clique in school, "The Plastics" (who are very aptly named, I might add). Caddie is quickly pulled into their backstabbing, cheating, lying ways, even though her conscience tells her that she needs to stay away and that these girls are total fakes and nothing but trouble.

As Caddie moves up the social ladder and eventually replaces Regina as the "it" girl, she realizes that she is miserable; she hates herself for the things she has done and for what she has become. She is now just like them.

The Plastics actually have a book called *The Burn Book*, which is full of pictures and hurtful lies and gossip about their classmates. When the book becomes public, it turns the school upside down, wounding everyone. In the end The Plastics are the most miserable of all. The popular Plastics become the bullies that everyone hates—all because of their big mouths. The trouble started not with what they *did* to other students but with what they *said*.

In Ephesians 4:29 the Word of God says, "Don't use foul or abusive language. Let everything you say be good and helpful, so that your words will be an encouragement to those who hear them" (NLT). How's that for a challenge? Talk about weighing every single thing you say. Notice that this verse doesn't say, "Let *most* things you say be good and helpful"; it says, "Let *everything* you say be good and helpful." I know that, for me, this seems almost impossible. But we all know that in Christ all things are possible.

Tips for Taming the Mighty Tongue

We'll talk in the following chapter about getting to the heart of the matter when it comes to controlling our tongues, but for now I'd like to offer you a few practical tips for keeping your tongue tamed.

When Gossip Starts, Zip It Up!

There is nothing more powerful than a little silence. If your friends insist on bringing up some juicy stuff, just sit there and don't say a word. If they ask you what's up, tell them you're practicing Tongue Control 101, based on Proverbs 17:27–28: "A truly wise person uses few words; a person with understanding is even-tempered. Even fools are thought to be wise when they keep silent; when they keep their mouths shut, they seem intelligent" (NLT). Now, I'm not saying you're a fool, but we could all glean something from this verse. Trust me, I've had someone use this tip on me before, and the silent treatment is very convicting to the gossiper!

Pretend It's Opposite Day

Whenever you feel a little bullet about to escape your mouth, force yourself to turn it into a positive comment. For example, maybe you're about to say to someone, "I really don't appreciate you liking the same guy I like. I claimed him first!" Instead, how about saying, "The shirt you are wearing is really cute. Where did you get it?" Strive to find a positive and helpful comment, even if it's against your nature at first. Some people might call this tip being fake; I say it's practicing self-control, which is one of the fruits of the Spirit, mind you!

Pray for Your Enemies

This is one of those things that really stinks when you first start doing it. I mean, let's be honest. Who wants to pray for someone who makes your life miserable? But let me tell you, there is something to it. Not only does praying for your enemies soften your heart, but in time, your kindness can affect the other person too. Prayer is your own secret weapon, and it's available to all girls of grace, thank goodness. It's also very handy, since there is no assembly required!

Consider Yourself

What I mean is, consider how what you are about to say would make you feel if it were spoken to you. If it would be helpful to you, then fire away. If not, it's probably better left inside your mouth.

It's a Daily Process

I know this all sounds wildly impossible to actually live up to, but the fact is, taming the mighty tongue is a daily process that takes time and attention. I promise, though, it will be worth the effort. Slow down and think about your own speeding bullets. Remember this verse from Psalm 34:12–14: "Do any of you want to live a life that is long and good? Then watch your tongue! Keep your lips from telling lies! Turn away from evil and do good. Work hard at living in peace with others"(NLT).

I know I want a life that is long and good. Don't you? Sounds like we now know the secret, so let's get to taming!

Do My Words Hurt or Heal?

Opening Scripture: Read James 1:26. Ask God to speak to you today as you study His Word.

☆ **Think before You Speak:** If you're like most girls, your words just come out. You freely express your thoughts and feelings. Your sister stains the shirt she borrowed from you, and you let her have it. Your brother gets on your nerves, and you respond in a less-than-kind way. It's so much easier to just let our mouths run and run—rather than weighing our words before we speak.

What's your experience? When we are stressed or irritated, we are less likely to think before we speak. What are your words like when you are stressed? ____

____

____

What does the Word say? Now look back at James 1:26. What does the verse teach about someone who doesn't "keep a tight rein on his tongue"? ____

____

____

Think about it: Worthless! That is a very strong word. It's so easy to think that sinning with our mouths is no big deal. But God says that when our words don't honor Him, we are fooling ourselves and our "religion is worthless." Do you seriously desire for your words to please Him?

- ❑ Sometimes.
- ❑ No, I don't want to change.
- ❑ Yes, my prayer is that God will help me tame my tongue.
- ❑ ____

Why do you think God puts such a high priority on what we say?

____

____

☆ Words Are a Window to the Heart

What does the Word say? Read Matthew 12:34. What does this passage teach about where our words come from? ____________________

____

____

Think about it: Have you ever said something mean and then later wondered where it came from? Matthew 12:34 teaches that hateful words reveal what's inside our hearts. While we often focus on outside appearance and actions, God cares the most about what's inside. He desires for our hearts to be filled with love for others. When you find that your words are mean, take some time to examine your heart. You may need to let God do open-heart surgery on you.

What's your experience? Based on the words you speak, what kind of grade do you think God would give your heart?

- ❑ U: Unsatisfactory behavior
- ❑ N: Needs improvement
- ❑ S: Satisfactory
- ❑ ______________________________

Chances are that you don't have a Burn Book like the one shown in the movie *Mean Girls*, but can you imagine if every hurtful word or lie you had ever spoken was written in a book? Would your book be small like a pamphlet or huge with several volumes? ____________

____

Think about it: A Burn Book can be destroyed, but the effects of hurtful words can last a lifetime. You may remember the childhood saying "Sticks and stones can break my bones, but words will never hurt me." While this is a cute rhyme, it's not necessarily true. A physical bruise or cut may heal, but the pain brought from careless words can last forever.

✯ Things to Guard Against

1. Gossip

What's your experience? Has there ever been a time when you have been hurt by gossip? Describe the situation. How did you feel? ________

____

____

Describe a time when you took part in gossip. What were the results?

____

____

____

What does the Word say? Maybe as far as you could see, no one got hurt. It's easy to trick ourselves into thinking that a little gossip is OK. But it's not! Gossip can have devastating consequences. It is a sin against God and against those He has called us to love. Read Proverbs 17:9. What does this verse say happens as a result of gossip?____________

____

____

2. Loose Lips

What's your experience? Have you ever struggled with loose lips? Maybe you've said something without thinking, and the damage has been done. If so, describe what happened: ___________________________

____

____

Think about it: Have you ever said, "I take that back" after saying something mean? Well, it's important to remember that you can't take something back once you've said it. We can ask for forgiveness, but we can never rewrite history. The results of our words, either good or bad, start the moment we speak them.

What's your experience? Can you remember a time when someone hurt you with his or her words? Even though it may have happened years ago, you can probably remember where you were and the person's tone of voice. Describe the situation and how you felt. __________

____

____

____

3. Lies

What's your experience? Have you ever told a "little white lie" to escape some trouble or make yourself look better?

- ❑ Never. (If so, are you lying now?)
- ❑ Yes, I really struggle with this.
- ❑ Yes, but it's no big deal.
- ❑ Yes, and I want to stop.

What does the Word say? Now read Proverbs 6:16–17. How does God feel about lying? ____

____

____

Think about it: God puts lying in the same category as "hands that shed innocent blood." In our human minds, murder seems so much worse than lying. But God doesn't weigh sin the same way we do. All sin is serious to Him, and it should be that way to us too.

☆ **Change Is a Daily Process:** Taming the tongue is a lifelong battle. It's not going to happen in a day, a week, or even a year. Just like taming a wild animal, controlling our tongues happens gradually over time. The more you consciously choose to cooperate with God in the area of tongue control, the more you will see positive results. You'll recognize times when you hold your tongue instead of speaking your mind. You'll tell the truth and resist lying. As God changes your heart, your words will change too. Let's look at some practical ways to surrender our tongues to God's control.

1. Pray. The first step to changing the hurtful words we say is prayer. Before you speak to anyone else each day, ask God to help you rely on Him for strength in controlling your tongue. Ask Him to help you use your words to build others up instead of tearing them down. Pray that He will change your heart so that what comes out of your mouth reflects His love and character. And when you do mess up, confess your sin and then move on.

2. Memorize the Word. As we have seen, when our minds change, so do our words. That's why it's so important to mentally "chew on" the Word of God. Write out some verses that deal with the mighty mouth and keep them handy. Memorize them when you're taking a shower or exercising.

Fill in the blanks:* Read Psalm 34:12–13, and fill in the missing words.

* Use the New International Version for the "Fill in the blanks" sections.

"Whoever of you ________ ________ and desires to see many ________ days, ________ your ________ from ________ and your lips from ________ ________."

3. Ask for help. I don't mean join the support group Bigmouths Anonymous, but you will find that taming the tongue is easier if you don't go it alone. Share with a Christian friend or youth leader your desire to change. Ask her to pray with you and hold you accountable. You may even want to set up a "no-gossip" rule with your friends. When the conversation heads toward gossip, you may want to say a code word you've agreed on with your friends that reminds you to change the subject.

✝ **Living the Word:** Read Proverbs 10:19–21.

• According to this passage, what happens when there are many words? ____

____

• What practical steps are you going to take so that you learn how to hold your tongue? ____

____

• Reread verse 21. How can the "lips of the righteous nourish many"?

____

____

____

Do My Words Hurt or Heal?

• Recall a situation where someone else's words "nourished" you. What did that person say, and how did his or her words affect you?

• Describe a time when God used your words to nourish someone else.

• Write out a prayer asking God to help you use your words to help others as opposed to hurt them. He is willing to help you change.

Mouth management doesn't
start with the mouth at all;
it starts with the heart.

The godly think before speaking;
the wicked spout evil words.
Proverbs 15:28 NLT

Mouth Management

Mouth management. Hmm. Interesting term, but what exactly does it mean? We talked in the previous chapter about the negative effects of a loose tongue and saw that most of us girls have a tendency to "gab to jab"! But how do we change what we've been doing for so long? How do we learn to manage our mouths?

The interesting thing is, mouth management doesn't start with the mouth at all. It starts with the heart. Jesus said in Luke 6:45, "For out of the overflow of his heart his mouth speaks." This means that whatever is in your heart just kind of bubbles up and comes out of your mouth! This can be good—or bad—depending on what's in your heart.

Fortunately, God did not leave us alone in the task of guarding our hearts. He's made controlling our hearts and tongues a team effort. So who exactly makes up this team? You, Jesus, and the Holy Spirit. Only with their help do we have the power to override the temptation for jab gabbing!

The Dream Team

It's amazing that two members of the Godhead (Jesus and the Holy Spirit) actually live inside of us. Talk about *dream team*! But does Jesus *really* live in your heart? The Bible says He does: "Christ lives in you, and this is assurance that you will share in his glory" (Colossians 1:27 NLT). But let's back up a minute. Before Christ can live in us, the Bible says we must believe in Jesus as the Son of God and receive Him. If you have never confessed to God that you desire Jesus to be Lord of your life, you can turn to pages 172–73 to find out how.

The first and most important step to mouth management is getting Jesus into your heart. And when Jesus lives in your heart as a "landlord," your heart will be well managed, and you'll stand a lot better chance of using your words wisely—to heal and not to hurt!

The second member of your team is the Holy Spirit. 1 Corinthians 6:19 says, "Your body is the temple of the Holy Spirit, who lives in you and was given to you by God" (NLT). One way to tell whether the Holy Spirit is really living in your heart is to check to see if His fruit is in your life.

When you look at the list of the Spirit's fruit in Galatians 5:22–23, it's amazing how many of them are tied directly to our speech. Have you ever noticed that? Look how some of the fruit of the Spirit can be directly tied to the words we say (or don't say!):

- Love—telling those who are closest to us that we love them
- Joy—speaking cheerfully to encourage those around us
- Peace—helping to resolve conflicts
- Patience—knowing when it's better *not* to speak but rather wait
- Faithfulness—being a loyal friend, with no backstabbing
- Self-control—again, knowing when to hold back

All of these traits are evidence to the rest of the world that God lives in our hearts.

Now that you've met your other team members, you're ready to move to the next step, which is taking an honest look inside your heart and cleaning it up so that what bubbles out is *good.*

A Look Inside

Even with the dream team living inside your heart, you still have to make your own choices about how you manage your mouth. And this means managing your thoughts before you speak. The only way to manage your thoughts is to manage your heart—and this starts with honest self-examination.

Even though examining your heart can be uncomfortable (oh, all right—it is sometimes downright *painful*), you have to assess what's there before you can clean up your thoughts and speech. You need to take an honest look at yourself so you can discover why you do the things you do and say the things you say.

The Gift of Gab—Shelley

I've always loved to kid around and crack jokes, many times at someone else's expense. When I consider my attempts to get laughs, I have to chalk a lot of it up to my personality. I've always been this way—loud, boisterous, joking all the time. Heather says that I say the stuff that other people think but would never say. (I'm not sure that's always a good thing, however.) I just genuinely love making people laugh.

Lately I've come to believe that my desire to make others laugh is really a gift from God—and I know I should use it carefully and wisely. But I never really thought of it as a gift until I read Frank Peretti's book *No More Bullies*.

Author Frank Peretti is best known for his book *This Present Darkness*, but his lesser-known book *No More Bullies* has some of the best material on the subject of bullies that I've ever read. In it he says: "God says that it is right to respect my fellow man, to love him, to care for him, and to protect him. It is wrong to abuse, tease, taunt, intimidate, hurt, harass, or violate anyone. Taking it a step further, to demean another person is sin. When we indulge in such practices, we are doing so in direct disobedience to our Lord Jesus Christ."[1] I love his directness, don't you? I mean, let's call a spade a spade. When we demean anyone, we are a sinner at her worst! This is why it's so important to continually keep our hearts in check—so we won't commit these sins against God. How we relate to others is serious business and needs to be treated as such.

Toward the end of that book, I read something that really changed me, forever I hope. Peretti tells about a bully he attended junior high school with who was nicknamed Mr. Muscles. Mr. Muscles used his physical strength to push people around. Peretti says that the bully was completely misusing his gift from God, and luckily, Frank got his courage up enough to tell him so. He told him, "*Any* gift you receive from God is not for yourself, but for others. The strong are to protect the weak; those with abundance are blessed so they can help the needy; the smart and the wise are gifted to help the befuddled and foolish."[2]

When I examine my heart and think about my gift of humor, I am totally convicted by this thought. How dare I ever use my gift to hurt others, all for a stupid laugh or to make myself seem funny! My gift of humor is not even *for* me; it's for those around me! Just like Mr. Muscles was there to *protect* the weak, not to bully them. I had never thought of it that way before. The fact that we even *can* talk should be considered a gift—a gift to be used for the gain of others not of ourselves.

More Heart Examination

Most people probably wouldn't know this about me, but if I were to be honest, I'd have to say that I deal with jealousy in my heart. If I were to really get to the bottom of things, the reason I may not use my mouth to compliment someone when I should is because of my own jealous pride. It's the weirdest thing, but I have trouble paying people compliments and building them up. I have no idea why. The only thing I can figure is that I'm dealing with some kind of deep-seated envy in my heart. Now that I think about it, I'm sure of it.

For example, I may look at a friend's new haircut, think it looks totally awesome, but then not say how good it looks. Isn't that ridiculous? Do I wish somewhere deep inside that *my* hair would look that great? Or maybe I just wish *she* didn't look so great. I really think that's it. How ugly is that!? How prideful of my heart! Seems to me that Shelley is taking up a little more room than Jesus and the Holy Spirit in my heart and that I need to move on over.

Lately I've really been working on saying the good things I think—and not just the negative things. For whatever reason, it's so much easier to speak the negative and to keep the positive inside. It should be the complete opposite, but there's that sin we have to deal with. I hate that! I mean, just to admit this about myself isn't easy, but at least it's the first step.

What's in Your Heart?

Is there something in your own heart that needs to be examined? Something that's bubbling up from your heart and coming out your mouth that is less than nice? I guess words really do show the real you. The Bible says it so clearly: "A good person produces good deeds from a good heart, and an evil person produces evil deeds from an evil heart. Whatever is in your heart determines what you say" (Luke 6:45 NLT). "For as he thinks in his heart, so *is* he" (Proverbs 23:7 NKJV).

Your heart is what God will look at in the end. I read a very sobering verse in Matthew that you may have never considered. I don't know about you, but it will make me inventory my heart before I use loose talk again: "You must give an account on judgment day of every idle word you speak. The words you say now reflect your fate then; either you will be justified by them or you will be condemned" (12:36–37 NLT). This verse is the ultimate reason for becoming a good "mouth manager."

It all begins, and ends, with our hearts.

STUDY GUIDE

Lord, Change My Heart

Opening Scripture: Ask God to speak to you in a specific way as you study His Word. Then read Luke 6:45.

Take a Look Inside: Have you ever hung up the phone or finished a conversation with someone and realized that you had just said a "zinger"? A zinger is one of those ugly things we say to or about someone that we should have just left unspoken. Zingers can slip out of our mouths before we even know what hit us. Where do they come from?

Fill in the blanks: Reread Luke 6:45 and fill in the missing words.

"The ________ man brings good things out of the ________ stored up in his ________, and the ________ man brings ________ things out of the evil ____________ up in his ________. For out of the overflow of his _________ his __________ speaks."

What does it mean? According to this verse, where do our words come from? ____

____

Think about it: When evil or unkind things come out of our mouths, what does that tell us about the condition of our hearts? __________

____

____

What's your experience? Has there ever been a time when you said something and then realized that the mean thing you said reflected what was going on inside of you? If so, describe the situation. ___________

____

____

____

☆ Praise or Poison?

What does it mean? Read James 3:7–10. What do you think verse 8 means when it says the tongue is "full of deadly poison"? ________

____

____

____

What two opposite things can come from the tongue?

- ❑ Happy and sad songs
- ❑ Screaming and whispering
- ❑ Praise and cursing
- ❑ Crudity and sophistication
- ❑ Rudeness and politeness

Think about it: Our tongues have the capacity for good and for evil. When we use our tongues to hurt others, it shows that our hearts need change. If you struggle with your words, you might need to take a long, hard look at what is going on inside. Maybe you have jealousy, like Shelley described, or bitterness or hate inside. Ask God to reveal what changes you need to let Him make in your heart so that your words will bless those around you.

☆ **We Are Responsible:** Have you ever noticed that in our society, no one wants to take personal responsibility for things they do wrong? We try to avoid consequences, and we certainly don't want punishment. It's the same way for the things people say. They want to say whatever they feel without suffering any cost. Well, God's Word says that life doesn't work that way. One day everyone who has ever lived will be held accountable for every word he or she has spoken. That's a sobering thought, isn't it?

What does the Word say? Read Matthew 12:36–37. According to this verse, for what will we be held accountable on the day of judgment?

- ❑ What we wore
- ❑ What we said
- ❑ Who we dated
- ❑ How much we prayed

Think about it: I don't know about you, but that verse really makes me think about some of the dumb things I've said. I wish I could erase some whole conversations I have had and some of the careless ways I have spoken to and about someone else.

What is your reaction to Matthew 12:36–37? ____________________

____

____

What do you think? Does knowing that you will have to give account for every word make you want to change the way you talk to and about others? Why or why not? ________________________________

____

____

Think about it: Maybe the thought of being responsible for every word makes you feel overwhelmed. You can remember all of the horrible things you've said, and it makes you want to give up hope of changing. You think you might as well move to a remote tropical island where you'll never speak to anyone again. Well, don't be discouraged. God will help you tame your tongue as you rely on Him and His power. You can move forward, knowing that He is quick to forgive and to help you change.

☆ **Filter Your Words:** Have you ever used a filter to separate two things? Maybe you were dividing liquid from something else or taking out something impure from the pure. In the same way, maybe you need to let God put a filter on your mouth. If so, the following verse is a great filter that will help you know what to say and what to leave unspoken. If our words don't fit the description in the verse, we should consider just keeping our mouths shut!

Fill in the blanks: Read Ephesians 4:29 and fill in the missing words.

"Do not let any ____________________ talk come out of your __________, but only what is __________ for building ____________ up according to their __________, that it may ____________ those who ______________."

What do you think? How can our words build others up? ___________

____

____

What's your experience? Has someone ever said something to you that built you up according to what you needed? If so, describe what that person said and how his or her words made you feel. ___________

____

____

Pray about it: Spend a few moments asking God to help you speak only words that will benefit those who listen to them. You may even want to add this prayer to your daily list. Pray this before you get out of bed in the morning and before you speak to anyone other than God.

✔ **Try This:** Use the space below to make a list of some positive ways you have used your words this week. Maybe you've helped a friend with a problem or a younger sibling with homework. Or you may have encouraged someone who was having a hard day. You might have told a friend about the love of Jesus and how to know Him better. These are some of the great ways we can use the gift of gab. Look over your list, and ask God to help you take advantage of more situations like these. ______________________________

____

____

____

What's your experience? After you finish that list, make a list of some of the negative ways you've used your words. Maybe you talked back to a parent or teacher or snapped at your little brother. You may have passed along a zinger to an unsuspecting friend. Or you may have spoken words of revenge when someone hurt you. ______________________________

____

____

____

____

Pray about it: Prayerfully read through this list, asking God to show if there is anyone He wants you to apologize to. If there is someone, or several people, call them today when you finish this lesson, and tell them you're sorry. Ask God to forgive you, and then pray that He will help you choose to hold your tongue the next time you're tempted to say something ugly. Remember, He is ready to forgive you and help you change from the inside out.

✝ **Living the Word:** Read Psalm 141:3.

• Rewrite this verse in your own words. ____________________

____

____

• What practical steps can you take this week to guard your words?

____

____

• Are there situations where you are more vulnerable to sinning with your mouth? If so, list those below. Then beside each one, write a way that you will be on guard against sinning with your words when you're in that situation. ____________________

____

____

____

____

• Now write Psalm 141:3 on a note card, and put it in your backpack or purse. Whenever you reach for your lip gloss or lipstick, read that verse. This will help you remember that your mouth can be used for good and evil. Choose to let God use it for good.

Did you know
that our hearts
actually teach our lips
what to say?

He who guards his mouth preserves his life, But he who opens wide his lips shall have destruction.
Proverbs 13:3 NKJV

Sanctified Gossip

With all this talk about how we're *not* supposed to talk, you may be wondering why God even gave you a mouth! It may seem the freedom of speech is more trouble than it's worth.

So what are we to do with these out-of-control contraptions, anyway? Is there anything we actually *can* say? Fortunately for us, girls, there is! I was privileged just a couple of months ago to hear Beth Moore speak at a Bible study in Houston, Texas. And she used a term in one of her illustrations that really got my attention. She talked about "sanctified gossip." When I heard that, I thought to myself, *Hmm, sounds like something I need to check into.*

Beth was speaking, as she often does, about the power of women in the Bible. In Mark 16 three women—Mary Magdalene, Mary the mother of James, and Salome—came to visit the tomb where Jesus had been put after His death on the cross. I'm sure you know the story. When the women arrived, they found that the large stone, which had covered the opening to the tomb, had been moved away; and Jesus was nowhere to be found. Instead, an angel greeted them: "You seek Jesus of Nazareth, who was crucified. He is risen! He is not here" (Mark 16:6 NKJV). Then he said, "But go and tell His disciples—and Peter—that He is going before you into Galilee" (v. 7 NKJV).

Did you get that? The angel commanded the women to *go* and *tell*. The stuff that girls love to do naturally! And besides that, the very first people who heard the greatest news that ever was or ever will be received by humankind—that Jesus Christ had risen from the dead—were three women. Not three men. Three women. Then just a couple of verses down, Jesus Himself first appeared after his triumph over death to Mary Magdalene, a woman who began to spread what Beth Moore so suitably calls "the first ever recorded case of sanctified gossip"!

My friends, it was not an accident that Jesus chose women first to get the word out. He knew we could do it! I believe it was completely by design. Telling the good news of Christ is by far the very best thing we can be spreading around. In fact, we are commanded to use our mouths to tell others about the awesome and noncondemning love of God.

People in this day and age really need to hear this news! The world we live in is so depressing sometimes that we can't even think straight. Using our mouths to witness and show God's love to others would be using them exactly the way they were made to be used.

Since most of us girls love to gossip so much, then let's do just that! But let's *sanctify* our gossip! Is that even possible? I think it is! Let's break it down. The word *gossip* means idle talk or rumor, especially about the person or private affairs of others. So obviously, this act in and of itself is a no-no. But *sanctified* means made holy, to purify or free from sin. So if we can take our "idle talk" about others and purify it—free it from sinful language—then all of a sudden, whatever we're saying will most likely bring glory to God instead of defame Him (and the person the comment is about). Sanctifying our words, along with our general "mouth management" as we discussed in the last chapter, begins in our minds and hearts.

Unsanctified Garbage

Did you know our hearts actually teach our lips what to say? "The heart of the wise teaches his mouth, and adds learning to his lips. Pleasant words are like a honeycomb, sweetness to the soul and health to the bones" (Proverbs 16:23–24 NKJV). This reminds us again that, sooner or later, whatever is in our hearts will inevitably bubble up out of our mouths. So it's our job to control the stuff that gets inside us. Just as eating junk food 24/7 will make us miserable, feeding our minds garbage will do the same. Chronic overeating of foods that are bad for you will make you gain weight and become unhealthy.

Likewise, chronically watching R-rated movies, reading sex-centered fashion magazines, and listening to music with raunchy lyrics will make you spiritually unhealthy.

Don't worry, I'm not going to preach to you or try to assume the role of your mom, but I am asking you to listen up for just a minute. *You cannot keep these kinds of habits, not even one of them, and be unaffected by them.* In some way, I promise, they will bring you down. I'm so tired of hearing girls say, "Oh, but I just like the groove; I'm not even listening to the lyrics." That is impossible, no matter how strong you are. Girls, we must run from every unholy thing we possibly can, because the fact remains, if we put the garbage in, it's gonna come out—either in our actions or in our words.

I wish we could have some sort of selective hearing or sight loss as Christians living in our world today. But we can't. What we read and watch and listen to affects us. Let's face it: we all like to read some of those magazines or watch shows like *The O.C.* I do too. But we can't sanctify the episodes or the movies before we feed them to our minds, so we're better off not even tempting ourselves. It's a struggle for me every single day. Should I watch? Should I not? Should I listen? Should I not?

If you can make the decision to make better choices about what you allow to go into your heart and mind, you will discover some amazing results. As you spend more time with God and less time with the world, your speech will begin to "sanctify" itself. You will have the power to compliment others, tell the truth, respect your parents, be gracious and thankful—the rewards are just endless. Proverbs 15:4 says, "A wholesome tongue is a tree of life, but perverseness in it breaks the spirit" (NKJV). I want my tongue to be a "tree of life," don't you?

Every Day Is a New Day

I love being a Christian for so many reasons, but I think one of the best things about it is the ability to have a fresh start every day. As Christians, if we confess our sins, God is faithful to forgive us and make us clean again (1 John 1:9). In this and the previous two chapters, some of you have probably been convicted about how you've been using your tongue. We've talked a lot about gossiping, bullying, and backbiting; and we all probably agree that it's wrong. But now it's time for us girls to come together and put a stop to it.

It's time to start spreading "sanctified gossip" and lifting up our brothers and sisters. It's time to focus on the positive impact our words can make today. Even thought we may not see the difference now, our words can affect lives for years to come. We have the girl power and the big mouths to do it!

Making a Fresh Start

Perhaps my favorite thing about the book I mentioned in the previous chapter, *No More Bullies*, is at the end of the book when Peretti gives us advice about making a fresh start:

> All it takes is a decision, a pivotal moment when you decide you will put a stop to the bullying and abuse and begin treating everyone who passes your way as a priceless, precious, miraculous creation of God, a person for whom Jesus Christ bled and died, a person who matters to God just as much as you do.
>
> The first step is to wake up to what you've done and what you may still be doing. Admit your sins honestly before God, ask him for forgiveness, and then declare that from this day forward, with God's help, your bullying and malicious teasing days are over. You will begin to treat every person as valuable, even sacred.[1]

Phew! Do you think we can do it? I challenge you to make a commitment to yourself and to God, along with whomever may have done this Bible study with you, that from this day forward, the words that flow from your mouth will be words of love and life.

Pray for me, and I'll pray for you, for this will not be an easy task. Remember that we have the power to speak life or death to someone's soul; it should be an easy choice. Happy gabbing!

STUDY GUIDE

Words of Life

Opening Scripture: Begin by reading John 3:16. This may be a familiar verse to you, so ask God to give you a heart to hear from Him in a new way today.

☆ **The Very Best News of All:** Have you ever received really great news? Maybe you made the team or received a call from Mr. Wonderful. You just had to tell your best friend what happened, and you couldn't wait. You tracked her down and shouted into the phone, "Guess what?" When good things happen to us, we just have to tell others—God made us that way.

Fill in the blanks: Reread John 3:16 and fill in the missing words.

"For ________ so ____________ the world that he ________ his _________ and only ________, that _________________ believes in him shall not _______________ but have _________________ life."

I can't think of any better news than this verse. We were separated from God because of the sin we chose, and God made a way for us to escape eternal death and punishment.

What does it mean? How did He make the way for us to have eternal life?

____

____

____

Think about it: Has there ever been a time when you shared God's free gift of eternal life? If so, describe when and what happened. If not, what words would you use to share this gift? (Turn to pages 172–73 for an example.) ____________________

____

____

____

What's your experience? Who was the first person to share the good news about Jesus with you? How did this person do it, and what did he or she say? ____________________

____

____

____

☆ **God's Heart for People:** Many of us have heard the story about Jesus's death on the cross so many times that we've become callous to it. We just take it for granted that the God of the whole universe became a man so He could suffer and pay the price for our sins. Maybe you saw Mel Gibson's movie *The Passion of the Christ*. If so, were you struck by the enormous suffering and pain that Jesus experienced on your behalf? It was unbelievable. Even though the movie was probably the most accurate representation of the crucifixion that most of us will ever see, the real event was far worse than any movie could depict. God loves people so much that He was willing to go to extreme measures to save us.

What does the Word say? Read 2 Peter 3:9. According to this verse, what is God's wish for all people?

- ❑ For them to read the Bible
- ❑ For them to stop littering
- ❑ For none of them to perish
- ❑ For them to learn about Jesus

What do you think? What does 2 Peter 3:9 show us about God's heart?

____

____

____

Pray about it: Spend a few minutes asking God to give you a burden for those who don't know Him. Ask Him to let you see people like He does and to give you the boldness to share with them so they can have a personal relationship with Him.

☆ **Sharing His Love:** Imagine that your friend found the cure for cancer. Maybe she was experimenting in chemistry class and somehow stumbled upon a rare formula that would heal everyone in the world suffering from the disease. You immediately realized that this was such great news that you needed to get the word out. You started to run off to call a national news station, but your friend stopped you. She whispered to you that she wasn't going to tell anyone and didn't want you to either. She had decided to keep the cure to herself. What would you think?

Obviously, you would be shocked to realize that she wasn't going to share this great news. Her selfish decision would cost many people their lives. It would be a great tragedy that the cure had been found, but the person who found it wouldn't share it.

Think about it: Isn't this the way it is with us and our salvation in Jesus? If we're Christians, we know the "cure" for sin and the way to have a saving relationship with God. Not sharing the message of eternal salvation through Jesus Christ is a far greater tragedy than not sharing the cure for cancer.

What does the Word say? Read Matthew 28:19–20. What are we, as Christians, commanded to do? ______________________________

____

____

____

☆ **Called to Be a Witness:** Have you ever watched a TV show that had a courtroom scene? If you have, you know that when a witness is called to the bench, he or she swears to tell "the truth, the whole truth, and nothing but the truth." The Bible calls on Christians to be witnesses to the truth as well.

What does the Word say? Read John 14:6. According to this verse, how does Jesus describe Himself? ______________________________

____

____

____

____

What do you think? What is the only way to have a relationship with God?

- ❑ Going to church
- ❑ Being born in a Christian family
- ❑ Having a relationship with Jesus Christ
- ❑ Being a good person

Think about it: Since Jesus is the truth, when we're called to share the truth as witnesses, that means we're sharing about Him. You don't have to know a bunch of Bible verses or fancy terms to be a witness. Witnesses simply tell others what has happened in their lives.

What's your experience? If you were to share with an unbeliever what God has done in your life, what would you say? Take some time to write about your life before you became a Christian, when you did become a Christian, and what your life has been like since. ______________

____

____

____

____

____

____

____

✔ **Try This:** Take some time to find some Bible verses that tell about the love of Jesus. Two to include are John 3:16 and John 14:6 from this lesson. Now write these verses on a front or back page in your Bible so that when you have a chance to share with someone about God's love, you'll easily find them. You may also want to copy them on a note card to slip in your backpack or purse.

✝ **Living the Word:** Read Matthew 5:14–16.

• What do you think verse 14 means by "you are the light of the world"? ____

____

• In what ways can you let your light shine so that others want to know more about Jesus? ______________________________

____

____

• List one person you are going to share Jesus's love with this week. Now write a prayer asking Him to prepare his or her heart to hear—and to prepare your heart to be a witness of the truth. ____________

____

____

____

____

____

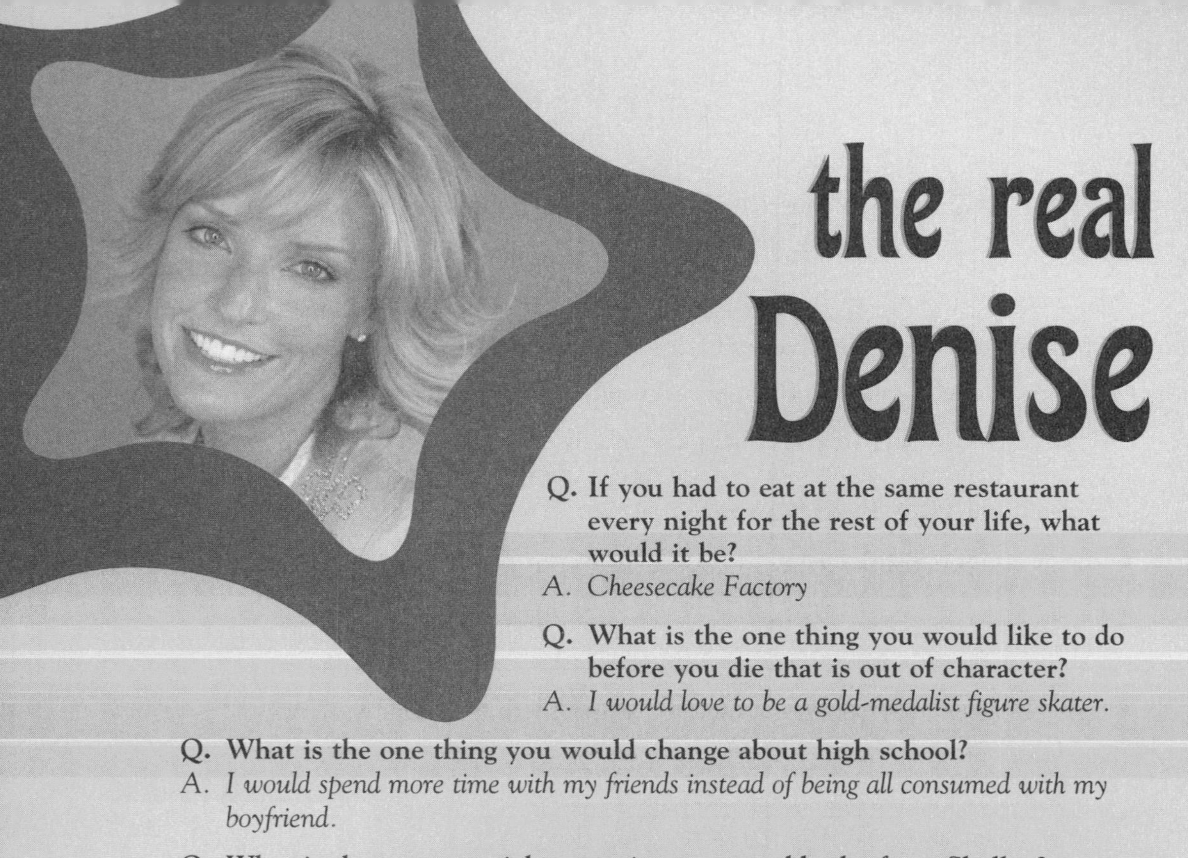

the real Denise

Q. If you had to eat at the same restaurant every night for the rest of your life, what would it be?

A. *Cheesecake Factory*

Q. What is the one thing you would like to do before you die that is out of character?

A. *I would love to be a gold-medalist figure skater.*

Q. What is the one thing you would change about high school?

A. *I would spend more time with my friends instead of being all consumed with my boyfriend.*

Q. What is the one material possession you would take from Shelley?

A. *Her Four Seasons Hotel mattress and box spring, along with her Frette sheets . . . nothing but LUSH!!*

Q. What characteristic do you love most about yourself?

A. *My bubbly personality.*

Q. What is the most embarrassing thing about yourself?

A. *I have ugly feet . . . bunions and all.*

Q. What is the one thing you tried out for and never made?

A. *I tried out for the Opryland Theme Park stage show and got the big fat NO!!*

becoming who YOU really are

God has created you with
your own unique set of gifts and
abilities, your own personality,
and your own special look.

I praise you because I am fearfully and wonderfully made; your works are wonderful, I know that full well.
Psalm 139:14

If the Shoe Fits, Wear It

It's amazing how much our closets reveal about who we are. The kinds of clothes we wear are almost like a uniform—you know, like the uniforms doctors, policemen, soldiers, and others wear to show the world who they are. What you wear makes a statement about who you are.

Take a look inside your closet. What kind of clothes do you see? Sporty? Trendy? Preppy? Casual? Do you have cheerleader outfits, basketball clothes, or tights and leotards for dance class? Do you choose comfort over fashion or the other way around? We all have different styles and ways of doing things.

In the same way, each of our hearts has its own closet as well. As we go through this chapter and the next two chapters, I want each of you to open wide the closet doors of your heart and take a good look at yourself. Don't worry. No one else will see. Just you and God, alone. And He loves you just the way you are right now—even if your heart's closet isn't in perfect order. I don't know anyone's that is! In this chapter we'll talk about *discovering* who God designed you to be and then *becoming* that beautiful girl of grace.

Speaking of girls of grace, it amazes me every day how different the four of us in Point of Grace are. Just taking a look at each of our closets will show you some of our differences. For instance, if you were to look in Shelley's or Leigh's closet, you would find them to be very neat, tidy, and organized. Shelley's clothes are organized by seasons, then divided by pants, skirts, shirts, etc. Leigh's would be set up in a similar way but color-coded as well. Now, Heather's or mine would look quite different. *Messy* would be Shelley's choice word for our closets. Mine might look a little more organized than Heather's, but let's just say that organization is not either of our strengths. Even when I do manage to clean out my closet a bit, it is a disaster within a week.

Besides our neatness—or lack thereof—our closets also show our differences by the kinds of clothes you'd find in them. In my closet you'd find a wide variety: golf clothes, singing clothes, take-the-kids-to-the-park clothes, and trendy stuff. Now, Shelley's closet would have a little less variety, and her clothes would be more classic and traditional. I have these crazy high-heeled black, long boots that Shelley would never want to wear. She has some beautiful classic sling-backs that I would probably never find anything to go with.

Just as our closets are different, so are our personalities. I'm hyper, bouncy, competitive, and always want to be on the go. Heather is laid back, a deep thinker, and takes things in stride. It takes a lot to stress her out. Shelley is in control and a great leader. She always knows how to motivate the rest of us. Leigh is the encourager, always wanting to help out where she is needed. She is a very faithful and devoted friend. I love how God chose to make us all unique. "For we are His workmanship, created in Christ Jesus for good works, which God prepared beforehand that we should walk in them" (Ephesians 2:10 NKJV). Each of us was created by God, but we all have our own shoes to walk in.

Discover Your SHAPE

Just like God has made the four of us different in Point of Grace, He has created you with your own unique set of gifts and abilities, your own personality, and your own special look. In fact, the Bible says that God actually shaped you, He formed you to be just whom He wanted you to be: "Your hands shaped me and made me" (Job 10:8). You were shaped by the God of the universe. But how many girls are satisfied with the shape God has given them? Even the most beautiful models say they would like to change something about themselves. Especially in America we are obsessed with our shape. The epidemic of eating disorders proves this.

But the truth is, God has shaped you in a unique way to serve Him. He has special things in mind for you. In the book of Isaiah, God says, "The people I formed for myself that they may proclaim my praise" (43:21). It's pretty hard to broadcast God's praises when we aren't happy with the way He created us. But we can become happy with how He's created us when we understand the beauty of our own unique SHAPE. In Rick Warren's book *The Purpose Driven Life*, he makes the word *shape* into an acronym.

Spiritual gifts

Heart

Abilities

Personality

Experience

You have been given each of the features above—hand-selected by God just for you—to be used for Him. Let's take a minute to look inside the closet of who God created you to be.

Spiritual Gifts

According to Rick Warren, spiritual gifts are special gifts given only to Christians and given for the express purpose of serving God. Here's how the apostle Paul explains it in Ephesians: "Christ gave each one of us the special gift of grace, showing how generous he is. And Christ gave gifts to people—

he made some to be apostles, some to be prophets, some to go and tell the Good News, and some to have the work of caring for and teaching God's people. Christ gave those gifts to prepare God's holy people for the work of serving, to make the body of Christ stronger" (4:7, 11–12 NCV).

God has given you spiritual gifts too. You may have the gift of making people feel comfortable or the ability to see into people's hearts and sympathize with their hurts. Your gift might be encouragement or generosity or sharing your faith. Maybe you have the gift of organization or leadership. Whatever gift God has given you, you can be sure that He intends that you use it for Him. Sometimes it takes us awhile to figure out what our spiritual gifts are—and that's OK. Ask God to show you where you fit in. Ask some of your friends or teachers where they think you fit in. You'll figure it out with a little time, prayer, and patience.

Heart

When we talk about *heart*, we're talking about what you love to do, what you're passionate about. Think about it for a minute. What do you love to do? What makes your heart beat fast? What are you passionate about? When you answer these questions, you'll know a little more about the person that God created you to be and a little bit more about how you fit into His plan.

Abilities

Pastor Warren says that your *abilities* are "the natural talents you were born with."[1] When you were born, you had in your genes the ability to do certain things well. What are you good at? What comes natural to you? Some people have a hard time coming up with an answer to these questions, but studies have shown that the average person has five hundred to seven hundred different skills and abilities. That's a lot! Even if you only tap into a fraction of yours, what a difference you could make! "Whatever you do, do it all for the glory of God" (1 Corinthians 10:31).

Personality

God has purposely created different kinds of personalities—and all of them are valuable and needed.

I read a book several years ago titled *Personality Plus* by Florence Littauer.[2] I highly recommend that you read it too. In it Florence explains the four main personality types and helps us recognize and be thankful for our own uniqueness. She even includes a few fun personality tests to help you understand yourself a little better.

The first thing you have to understand is that there are no right or wrong personalities. Our God is a God of variety, and He created different personality types on purpose and for a purpose. "Now there are different kinds of spiritual gifts, but it is the same Holy Spirit who is the source of them all. There are different kinds of service in the church, but it is the same Lord we are serving. There are different ways God works in our lives, but it is the same God who does the work through all of us" (1 Corinthians 12:4–6 NLT). Your particular personality type is a gift from God. It may need some refinement and maturing, but your basic personality is *good*.

Experience

Our life experiences—good and bad—also play a big part in shaping us into who we are. You've had all kinds of experiences: family experiences and educational experiences, job experiences, and spiritual experiences. All of these have helped shape you into the person you are. And you've also had painful experiences. And in a strange way, our painful experiences can end up being a blessing—if we let them.

Just think about it a minute: it's the painful experiences that most prepare us to help someone else, because when we've experienced pain, we better understand the pain of others. Paul put it this way: "Praise be to the God and Father of our Lord Jesus Christ, the Father of compassion and the God of all comfort, who comforts us in all our troubles, so that we can comfort those in any trouble with the comfort we ourselves have received from God" (2 Corinthians 1:3–4). See what he's saying? When you hurt and are comforted by God, then you are able to pass that comfort on to other hurting people.

And besides helping us be more sympathetic to others in pain, if we let it, pain can

also help us move closer to God. In addition to that, it gives us a new perspective of what's truly important in life. So you see, our experiences—even the painful ones—are part of what shapes us into who we are.

Be What God Made You to Be

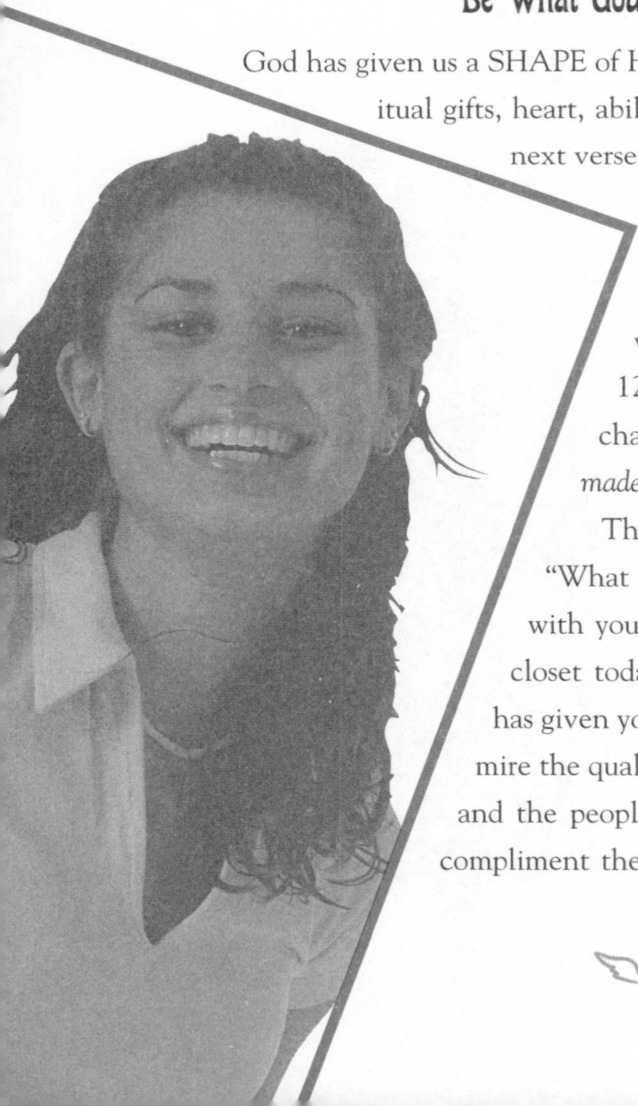

God has given us a SHAPE of His own choosing—He has given us spiritual gifts, heart, abilities, personality, and experiences. This next verse says it all: "Since we find ourselves fashioned into all these excellently formed and marvelously functioning parts in Christ's body, let's just go ahead and be what we were made to be" (Romans 12:5–6 The Message). That is a beautiful challenge: *just go ahead and be what God made you to be.*

There's an old Danish proverb that says, "What you are is God's gift to you; what you do with yourself is your gift to God." Dig into your closet today. Pull out those unique qualities God has given you, and wear them proudly. It's OK to admire the qualities God has put in the closets of others and the people He has shaped them to be—even to compliment them for it. We all need to be noticed for our own style and personality. But be content with the beautiful girl of grace God has called *you* to be.

So wear whatever "shoe" God has given you. Don't try to cram your foot into a shoe that doesn't fit. Don't be like Cinderella's older sisters, who wanted so badly to be someone they weren't that they tried to stuff their feet into a too-small shoe.

You can choose to develop the talents and skills that go with your personality and become a truly wonderful, well-developed woman; or you can struggle in vain to try to develop talents and skills that belong to someone else. But that shoe will never fit. Oh, you can force it and fake it and try to wear shoes that just don't fit, but your feet will *always* hurt—and you definitely will not live happily ever after.

Who He Made Me to Be

Opening Scripture: Ask God to speak to you in a specific way as you study His Word today. Then read Psalm 139:13–14.

Accepting Who God Made You to Be: If you could be anyone in the world, who would you be? Would you be a famous actress or a model? Or maybe you would morph into someone who goes to your school. She doesn't seem to have any problems, has the perfect wardrobe, and has never struggled with her weight. Isn't it easy to look at someone else's life and think that she has it made? We do it all the time. When we flip through magazines, we wish we could have the bodies of the models on the pages. Watching our favorite TV shows reminds us of how funny and stylish we don't feel. When we listen to what the world says, it's easy to forget that we are God's unique creations. That's why it's important that we look to His Word to define who we are.

What's your experience? Have you ever longed to be someone else rather than who God made you? If so, who? ______________________

Even this person would want to change something about herself. The key isn't altering who we are, but accepting and embracing it.

Fill in the blanks: Reread Psalm 139:13–14 and fill in the missing words.

"For you ________ my inmost being; you ______ me together in my __________ womb. I praise you because I am _________________ and ____________________ made; your works are ____________, I know that full well."

What do you think? How does that verse make you feel about yourself?

- ❑ Excited that God made me special
- ❑ Sad that I have never known this before
- ❑ It doesn't really make a difference in how I feel
- ❑ ____

What's your experience? Have you ever received a handmade present? Maybe someone knitted you a sweater or painted you a picture. Or perhaps someone wrote you a song or poem. If so, how did you feel about the gift? ____

____

____

Think about it: Psalm 139 says that God "knit" you. What an amazing thought: the God of the universe has especially designed you! He could have spoken the word and made all people the same. But He didn't. He made you a one-of-a-kind so that He could use you in the unique plan He has for your life.

☆ **Designed for a Purpose:** Acts 17:26–27 teaches that God even determined where and when we would live. According to these verses, why did God create us?

- ❑ To witness to others
- ❑ To love others

❑ To seek Him

❑ To serve Him

What do you think? God created you so that you would seek Him and know Him. How well are you fulfilling that purpose? ____________

____

When we know God, we learn more about His plans for our lives. We come to realize that God has designed each one of us with a unique SHAPE.

☆ **What SHAPE Are You?** I'm not talking about whether you are tall and thin or short and round or somewhere in-between. According to Rick Warren in *The Purpose Driven Life*, there are five things that go into making the SHAPE of who you are.

1. Spiritual gifts. God gives each Christian at least one spiritual gift so that we can use it to serve Him. It may take you a little while to figure out which ones you have; but the more you serve Him, the more your spiritual gifts will be revealed. Sometimes people take inventories that help them discover what their gifts are. Another way is to ask those who know us best.

What's your experience? Do you have any idea what spiritual gift or gifts you might have? If so, write them here. ________________________

____

____

What does the Word say? Read Romans 12:4–8. Why is it important that there are all kinds of gifts given to different Christians? ______________

____

____

Your gifts may not be the most visible gifts, like those of your pastor or youth leader, but they are just as important. Be sure to "open" them and use them.

2. Heart. What gives you the greatest joy? (And I'm not talking about shopping.) Maybe it's taking care of children or serving those less fortunate. You might have a desire to create art that glorifies God.

What do you think? List some of the passions of your heart. ______________

____

____

Think about it: Are you using these passions to serve Him? If you have a heart for children, then why not volunteer to work in your church children's program? What are some practical ways you can glorify God with the passions in your heart?______________________________

____

____

____

____

____

3. Abilities. You may not think you have them—but you do! Are you a fast runner or an especially loyal friend? Maybe you are good in science or can take really great pictures.

Think about it: List some of your abilities. ______________________

____

____

How can you use these abilities to honor God?________________

____

____

4. Personality. Look back at Psalm 139:13–14. Did you know that when God made you, He gave you a particular "bent" or personality? While your parents and environment have also shaped you, a lot of your personality was determined even before you were born. Are you laid back? Energetic? A leader? A thinker?

What do you think? If your best friend had to describe your personality in three words, what would she say? ____________________

____

5. Experience. Think back over your personal history from the time you were born until now. God can use all of the things that have happened to you, good and bad, to help others and honor Him. No one else has the exact same experiences you have.

Think about it: If you had to title the story of your life, what would it be?

___

___

☆ **God Wants to Use You:** Read 1 Corinthians 2:9. According to this verse, describe the plans that God has for those who love Him.

___

___

It's important to remember that His plans for you will be different than those for your best friend. So stop comparing yourself. You are a one-of-a-kind masterpiece. Ask God to help you see yourself that way.

Pray about it: If you struggle with seeing yourself as the treasure you are, commit to praying about it. You may want to pray back to God such scriptures as Psalm 139. The more you saturate your mind with the truth, the more you will see yourself for the unique creation you are.

✔ **Try This:** Find a recent picture of yourself and attach it to the center of a big piece of paper. Next, on the paper write your positive traits and abilities. You may want to include such info as you are a good listener (and draw an arrow to your ears) or that you have a great sense of humor. You can also include positive comments about your appearance. For instance, you may have strong arms, straight teeth, or shiny hair. Lastly, include some Bible verses that explain how special you are to God. You can include some from this lesson or look for others.

The next time you have a bad hair day, let this picture remind you that you are a handmade treasure.

✞ **Living the Word:** Read Jeremiah 29:11.

• According to this verse, describe the plans God has for you.

____

____

• What steps will you take to help you remember that you are God's masterpiece created with a special plan for your life? ____________

____

____

• Write a prayer thanking God for making you the way you are. Next, ask Him to use you in your generation to fulfill the purpose He has for you. ____

____

____

____

____

____

It's time to open up the closet, dig out that dirty laundry, and bring it to our "cleanser," Jesus Christ.

But if we confess our sins to him, he is faithful and just to forgive us and to cleanse us from every wrong.
1 John 1:9 NLT

Dirty Laundry

My closet is the last thing I would want you to see if you came to my house. It's the place I throw all of the stuff I don't want to deal with at the moment. Unfortunately, that's how I sometimes deal with the closet of my life.

From the time I was a little girl, neatness has not come naturally to me. The biggest arguments with my mother were over cleaning my room. I totally hated it. Cleaning took work, and my sanguine personality liked to play. So when I lost the battle and had to clean my room, the closet became the junk pile. I crammed so much stuff into my closet that I would have to shove the door closed with all my might. Well, I'm sure you can imagine what happened when my mom decided to put her life at risk by opening my closet door. *Avalanche!* Everything came tumbling out, and my room was messier than ever.

Closet Confessions

By looking at a CD cover or one of our posters, you might not know that I am a messy person. I try to look as good as I can. But I can definitely say that I have dirty laundry in the corners of my closet. And when I don't deal with it, things begin to stink. It's the same with my heart. When I don't deal with the troublesome issues in my life, my aroma is less like a rose and more like a clove of garlic. See if you identify with any of the "dirty laundry" I have stuffed back in my closet.

Closet Comparisons

One of the issues that piles up in the closet of my heart is *comparison*. For some reason, other people's closets always look better than mine. I end up making all kinds of assumptions about what others have in their closets. I assume they have it more together than I do, that their clothes are cuter than mine, that everything is in perfect style, and that everything fits perfectly.

You would think that I would have outgrown comparisons by now, but all that has changed is what I compare. In high school I thought, *She's prettier, skinnier, smarter, a better singer, or a better athlete than I am*. Now as an adult I think, *She's a better mom, she's a better wife, she has it all together, or she's more spiritual than I am*. Then there are the never-ending comparisons: *She's skinnier, has less cellulite, or has less wrinkles. How is it possible that she has had four kids and still looks amazing?*

Here's the problem. When I compare myself to someone else, I'm discontent with who I am and what I have. And as we said in the last chapter, God has made you who you are on purpose and for His purpose.

God does not intend for you to compare yourself to others; He intends that you look at yourself objectively, in light of who He has created you to be: "Each person should judge his own actions and not compare himself with others. Then he can be proud for what he himself has done" (Galatians 6:4 NCV).

The Bible actually says that you are a *masterpiece*! You are who God intended you to be! He wants you to be you—not someone else. "For we are God's masterpiece. He has created us anew in Christ Jesus, so that we can do the good things he planned for us long ago" (Ephesians 2:10 NLT). God had wonderful plans for you—plans that He began before you were even born.

Closet Fear

Fear is another one of those issues that I cram inside my closet, hoping it will just go away. When I was in the ninth grade, I had an experience that I allowed to affect me for years. I air-balled a game-winning free throw to lose against our rival team in basketball. I thought my heart was going to explode and never recover. But the next day at school, I put on my happy-girl smile and acted as if everything was fine. Yet from that point on, with every free throw, I lived in fear that I would miss again. Well, more often than not, I did miss, because I never let myself get past that moment.

Basically, I became a poor loser. You see, when I missed a shot, I would say to myself, "You stupid idiot, you knew you would miss that shot. You never should have played basketball in the first place. Next time you had better make it." Well, with that kind of attitude, do you think I made it?

Instead, I should have said to myself, "Although I don't like it when I miss, I realize that I can't make every shot. I noticed that my elbow wasn't in and that I didn't follow through my shot, so I'll practice those techniques this week and come to the game next week with more confidence." Then all next week, I should've stayed after practice a little and worked on my shot instead of grumbling to myself about what a loser I was.

To add to the messages in my own head, one of my coaches told me that I just couldn't "finish" and that I was a "choker." I made the mistake of believing her, and I even applied her words to other areas in my life—including my singing. When it was time for a solo, I lived in fear that I would mess up or crack on the most important part. Even today I struggle with that fear and have to keep turning it over to the Lord.

But as I grow as a Christian, I'm learning that the cure to fear is *trust*. Psalm 56:3 says, "When I am afraid, I will trust in you," and Isaiah 50:10 says, "Let him who walks in the dark, who has no light, trust in the name of the LORD and rely on his God." Those verses are worth memorizing! Get yourself a couple of three-by-five note cards and write these verses on them. Tape them to your mirror so you'll see them while you're getting ready in the morning. Repeat them until they are imbedded in your heart. Next time you feel afraid or as if you are walking alone in the dark, remember the words to these verses and replace fear with trust.

Closet Pleaser

Being a people pleaser is another one of those "dirty-laundry" issues that stinks up my closet. I didn't realize until a few years ago how much I was afraid of what people thought of me. Every decision and action I made was based on what people would think. When I came out of my closet in the mornings, I would put on a big smile and bubbly personality—whether I felt like it or not.

Where did we get the idea that Christians are always happy and doing great? I remember as a child having huge fights in the car on the way to church and then stepping into the parking lot and being all, "Great, how are you doing?" Do you relate?

Why is keeping up appearances so important to us, anyway? I guess it's because we want to fit in, we want everyone to like us, and we don't think they'll like us if we let them see our pain. So when we hurt, we slap a smile on our faces and pretend that everything is fine. And on top of that, we have the mistaken idea that as Christians, we have the responsibility to always appear joyful and happy.

But I now realize that being vulnerable to others and allowing them to see that I, too, have bad days gives them permission to share their pain with me.

And as I am open about my struggles, I can share about my Friend, Jesus, who stays by my side through it all. When I am humble enough to share the real me, I can share my need for a real Savior.

In her book *Deceived by Shame, Desired by God*, Cynthia Spell Humbert says this, "To admit that we have needs is not an admission of weakness, it's a confession of our humanity, we all have needs . . . that's the way God made us . . . and to admit that we have needs is not only truthful, it's beneficial."[1]

Closet Secrets

At every Girls of Grace conference, we get questions from girls who are struggling with deep, dark secrets. Sadly, these girls often hold their pain inside because they are afraid to ask for help. Let's take a closer look at these secrets.

No Fault of Your Own

Some of our dirty laundry is a result of what other people do to us and is no fault of our own. Some families hide awful secrets—alcoholism, sexual abuse, verbal abuse, or neglect. I can't speak from experience on this kind of secret pain, but I'd like you to hear the story of a friend of mine who can:

> I was abused by my father sexually, physically, and verbally for seven years. His abuse broke my heart, distorted my view of male authority figures and of God, and shaped my self-image into a victim mentality. I never told anyone about the abuse during those seven years; I even held the secret in

many years after. Holding this family secret caused much pain, which led to an eating disorder, severe depression, low self-image (suicidal thoughts), and a sexual addiction.

At the age of twenty-eight, I finally shined the light of truth on the dark secret that had bound me in chains for so many years. I finally found the courage to seek help and tell the truth. Now I'm learning to live in the light, and through counseling I've learned to talk about the pain I encountered. In doing this and in looking to the Author of my life, I now stand in victory—free of shame, guilt, and anger.

When I look back at those years of abuse, I wish I had told the secret—no matter what happened afterward. So this is my advice to you: if you have a secret like this, run and tell it to someone you trust, someone who can help you get out of the situation! Don't hold your secret in. Go to a teacher or pastor or counselor—someone who can help you.

Even though life has been a long road with much pain, confusion, and simply wondering, *why me?* I have learned that the journey is not a sprint, but rather a marathon that I have to keep training for. I have also learned that life comes in seasons of dry times, sunshine, fun times, and down times. These seasons still come, but

> in each season, God molds me into who He is calling me to be. I am learning to see God's picture in full color and large screen, for He has created me for a purpose to do, say, be, and live for Him.
>
> I have cried many hours, but I now know that God is always there watching, waiting, and catching every tear. I now see God as my loving father. His love has healed my heart, captured my heart, and has given me a beat that now beats after Him!

I'm proud of my friend for sharing her story and proud of her for finally getting help. I hope you heard her loud and clear when she advised those who are victims of abuse to seek out someone they can trust and ask for help. Even though I have no personal knowledge of this kind of abuse, I do know that it is *not* your fault. If you are a victim of abuse, you are not responsible!

But the abuse will not go away until it is brought into the light. The dirty laundry will continue to pile up, and the stench and the filth will grow until you are desperate for relief. And when we're desperate, we will try anything in the hopes of making life better—if just for one moment. But the actions we think will bring relief often only heap more harm upon ourselves. This "relief" may come in the form of drinking, cutting, drugs, sex, or eating disorders. All of which will lead to *avalanche*! Get help now.

The Result of Our Own Choices

We've talked about closet secrets that are totally outside our control, but there are some closet secrets that are the result of our own choices. And sometimes what starts out as a conscious choice spirals into addictions or entrapping behaviors that we *want* to get out of but feel we can't. You might be hiding a secret addiction to alcohol or drugs, or you might be entrapped in cutting, an eating disorder, or wrong sexual behavior. It's possible to hide an addiction to alcohol or drugs for a while, but eventually their power over you can severely affect your everyday life. You can hide an eating disorder for a while—until you are so sick that you need medical attention. And you can cut yourself for a while without anyone noticing, but this kind of secret is hard to keep. Cutting may seem to dull your inner pain temporarily; but eventually, you find that it no longer works. All of these secrets can lead to extreme danger and dysfunction.

Whatever problems our choices get us into, God has provided a way out. Scripture makes this promise: "The temptations that come into your life are no different from what others experience. And God is faithful. He will keep the temptation from becoming so strong that you can't stand up against it. When you are tempted, he will show you a way out so that you will not give in to it" (1 Corinthians 10:13 NLT). What an amazing promise! Whatever temptation you may be experiencing, God has promised a way out. This promise does a couple of things: on the one hand, it gives me tremendous hope; and on the other hand, it takes away my excuses.

Just like we make choices to begin harmful behavior, we can make choices to stop. Oh, I'm not saying that it's easy. It's not. It may be the fight of your life. But *choice* is one of the greatest blessings we have from God. Just like so many other gifts, we can use it for good or bad. Let's talk a minute about how you can use it to get help.

Getting Help

Just like there are stains in our clothing that won't come out in the washing machine—stains that require a professional dry cleaner—there are some problems in our lives that require professional help. There is no shame in getting help from a professional. Just as we go to medical doctors when we are physically sick, we should go to someone who can help when we are spiritually or emotionally sick.

But you can't get help until you are ready to tell someone that you need help. Talk to a trusted adult, a school counselor, a teacher, or other school official. If the first adult you talk to does not get you help, then go to another adult until you find someone to listen and to help you. You have the right to tell someone, and you have the right to expect help in getting this behavior stopped.

The most significant help we can ever get—whether our secrets are large or small—is found in the blood of Jesus. Only His blood can completely wash away the stains of our hurts, addictions, struggles, and sin. These words from one of my favorite hymns say it all:

Dirty Laundry

What can wash away my sins?
Nothing but the blood of Jesus.
What can make me whole again?
Nothing but the blood of Jesus.
Oh precious is the flow
That makes me white as snow.
No other fount I know.
Nothing but the blood of Jesus.

"If we walk in the light, as he is in the light, we have fellowship with one another, and the blood of Jesus, his Son, purifies us from all sin" (1 John 1:7).

It's time to open up the closet and, with His help and the help of someone who can walk with you, dig out that dirty laundry and bring it to our "cleanser," Jesus Christ. He is the only one who can truly begin the healing process. Don't you think it's time for the "stink" to go away?

STUDY GUIDE

I Am a Masterpiece

Opening Scripture: Ask God to teach you His truth today as you study His Word. Read Ephesians 2:10.

Who You Are According to God: If I were to ask you to describe yourself, what would you say? Would you say you are funny? Pretty? Smart? Mischievous? While many things would come to your mind, I doubt the word *masterpiece* would. When we run the tapes in our heads that tell us who we are, we too often tend to focus on the negative. We think of how we have a scar on our cheek or how we wish our hair were lighter or our hips thinner. We list the things we would change about ourselves. But if you were to ask God to describe you, do you know what He would say? Read on and see.

Fill in the blanks: Reread Ephesians 2:10 and fill in the missing words.

"For ___________ are God's _________________, ________________ in Christ Jesus to do ___________ works, which God prepared in __________ for ________ to ________."

What do you think? God's Word calls you His workmanship. Another way to say that would be you are His work of art. How does that make you feel?

- ❑ It makes me feel like a treasure.
- ❑ I don't feel anything because I can't believe it.
- ❑ It makes me want to see myself the way God sees me.
- ❑ ____

I Am a Masterpiece

Think about it: We have all struggled with seeing ourselves as His masterpieces. Why do you think it's so hard to believe what God's Word says about us? ____

____

____

☆ **Looking at Everyone but Him:** One reason we find it so hard to trust what God's Word says about us is true is that we continually look at others rather than at God. We've all done it. We find someone that we think is nearly perfect and think of all the ways she is better, thinner, smarter, and more "together" than we are. This kind of thinking takes our focus off of where it should be: on God and His purposes for our lives.

What's your experience? Think of a time when you compared yourself to someone else? What was the result? ______________________

____

____

What does the Word say? Read Galatians 6:4. What does this verse teach about comparing ourselves to others?

- ❑ It helps us feel better about ourselves.
- ❑ It gives us something to do when we're bored in class.
- ❑ God warns us against it.
- ❑ It's not that bad as long as you don't say it out loud.

Pray about it: Maybe you are realizing that comparison robs you of seeing yourself as the masterpiece He has made you to be. If so, take some time to pray that God would help you view yourself the way He sees you. You might want to memorize Ephesians 2:10 and pray that back to Him each time you feel tempted to compare yourself to others. The comparison habit won't go away overnight, but as you pray about it daily, you'll find that you're more likely to look at Him than at everybody else.

Fear Factor: Maybe you, like Denise, have struggled with fear. It seems that our world offers up many fears for us to choose from: fear of failing, fear of what other people think, and fear of the unknown.

What's your experience? What are some of your biggest fears? (It's OK. Don't be afraid to list them. Admitting you have fear is the first step to freedom. ____

____

____

What does it mean? Read Proverbs 18:10. What does this passage teach about the protection of the righteous when they come to God? ____

____

____

Think about it: The next time you find yourself wrestling with fear, look for a Bible verse that talks about trusting God. Read and memorize it. Then when fear pops its ugly head again, you will have the verse ready to pull out as ammunition. You can tell God that you have fearful thoughts and ask Him for the grace to trust Him through the situation.

☆ **"What Do They Think About Me?"** We've all been there. We walk into a room and wonder what everyone is thinking about us. (Most of the time, they aren't thinking of us at all, because they are thinking of themselves.) We are having a sad day; and when someone asks us how we are, we lie. We want to please people. We want to have a certain image, and what we say and do is determined by what will make others like us. While there is nothing wrong with wanting others to like us, our desire to please people shouldn't drive how we live. Pleasing God should be light-years more important to us than pleasing other people. So why is it often the other way around?

What's your experience? Have you ever let the fear of what others think about you change your behavior? If so, explain.____________________

____

____

What does it mean? Read Proverbs 29:25. What do you think this passage means by "a snare"?____

____

____

Instead of looking to other people, whom does this verse point to as trustworthy?____

Think about it: Do you want to be a God pleaser or a people pleaser? You'll probably need to make this decision every day. Maybe even every hour or minute. Determine that as His masterpiece, you will let God, not the world, determine who you become.

☆ **Let God Set You Free:** As you give over comparisons, fear, and people pleasing to God, you'll find it's easier to see yourself as the masterpiece He created. Maybe you have other things that hinder you from living as His one-of-a-kind work of art. There may be hurts and painful memories that you have never shared with anyone. Maybe you have an addictive habit, such as an eating disorder or cutting, that holds you back from seeing yourself as His treasure. Whatever it is, God can set you free. Come to Him honestly today, and let Him begin the process of freeing you from the inside out.

What does the Word say? Read John 8:32. When we live by God's truth, what is the result? ______________________________

What do you think? Are there areas in your life where you need God to set you free? If so, list some of them here. ____________________

____

____

✔ **Try This:** It's important to have people in our lives whom we can trust with private and often painful information. Make a list of some people whom you could confide in and who would treat what you share with great care and respect. If you can't think of anyone, put down the name of a youth leader, pastor, or teacher you know. ____

____

✝ **Living the Word:** Read James 5:16.

- What does this passage say we should do with others? ___________

____

____

- What will the result be? ___________________________

____

____

- What does James 5:16 say about prayer? _______________

____

____

- Will you ask someone to pray with you that you will start to see yourself as His loved and special masterpiece? If so, list her name here.

____

- If you have suffered some form of abuse and have never told anyone, this Bible study was written just for you. Look at the list of trustworthy people you made, and choose one person to tell today. If it is literally impossible to tell that person today, determine to do it tomorrow. Letting someone know what happened to you is the first step to healing. Will you take that step to get help today? ___________

If we truly want to have the closet
of our hearts designed by the great
Creator, Organizer, and Finisher,
we must spend time with Him.

So get rid of all the filth and evil in your lives, and humbly accept the message God has planted in your hearts, for it is strong enough to save your souls.
James 1:21 NLT

Closets by Design

One day I came home from a trip, and my husband had several brochures lying on the table. No, they weren't brochures of Hawaii, the Caribbean, or the Bahamas. They were brochures from interior closet designers. Sound exciting? Not really. But necessary. Stu had been at home a few days too long with my kids while I was on the road and had gotten tired of the mess.

Stu is the choleric personality—the one who is in control, likes organization, and is goal oriented—and he had a goal in mind: to organize our closet. Ugh! I'd rather just go get ice cream and forget about it. But I reluctantly set some meetings with different designers, and we decided to go with Closets by Design.

Deborah was a very nice lady—enthusiastic and energetic. She made me feel as if this would be an easy and fun task. We talked about my lifestyle—the need for easy packing and unpacking, what clothes I wore the most, and the easiest setup for putting things back where they belong. She then began to draw out what she felt would best fit our needs. We agreed on a plan, and they went to work. Finally the shelves were built and rods put up. Eventually the bill was paid, and Deborah was gone.

There was only one problem. Now I had to organize all of my things and put them back in the closet. Where was my enthusiastic cheerleader now? I was left to deal with all the "stuff." Thankfully, I have very organized friends who gave me some great tips. Some of these tips may come in handy for you, too.

1. *Separate your clothes into pieces you want to keep and pieces you don't*. I had to go through my clothes, piece by piece, and figure out what fit, what didn't, what looked good on me, what didn't, what had stains that weren't going away, what needed alterations, and what couldn't be fixed. Then there were the shoes that I had to decide if they were in style or not. Was it OK to get rid of an old Point of Grace outfit? All of those questions.

2. *Divide the "don't-keep" pile into "throw-away" and "give-away" piles*.

3. *Divide the "keep" items into sections: pants, jeans, skirts, boots, heels, etc*.

4. *Put everything in the closet accordingly*.

5. *Add pieces to make wardrobe complete*. This was my favorite part, by far!

Understand that this was an extreme task for me. None of it came easy, and I didn't consider it a fun pastime. I could only bear it because of what my husband promised I could do if I completed this task: he said I could go shopping and add to what I had to complete my wardrobe!

Well, I have to tell you what a wonderful feeling I had when it was all done. I realize that it will take work for me to keep it clean, and we will see how long it lasts; but hopefully I have learned that it's much better to deal with things at the moment than to let them build up.

Now, how does this fit in to your closet and your story? Let's see.

Take a Personal Inventory

Just like you sometimes take an inventory of your closet and get rid of the crummy, outdated stuff, you can take a personal inventory of yourself and take away some of the bad and add some good. Here are some ideas of how to go about making your life a "Closet by Design."

Step 1: Remember That You Are Designed by God

"The LORD who created you says: 'Do not be afraid, for I have ransomed you. I have called you by name; you are mine'" (Isaiah 43:1 NLT). God is the one who shaped you. He knows everything there is to know about you and has designed you with purpose. People and circumstances have added to the original design and made it a

little messy, but God's plan for you is still intact. There's a big difference in my closet organizer, Deborah, and God. God not only designed your closet, but He will be the friend who helps you inventory, clean, and continue to grow the wonderful you He designed you to be.

Step 2: Figure Out What's Within Your Control and What's Not

We waste all kinds of energy and emotion trying to change things that are totally beyond our control. We can't control our family, the circumstances we were born into, how tall we are, or the skin type we have. We can't change our basic personality type or the gifts and skills we were born with. But there are a *lot* of things we can control. So let's get to work.

Step 3: Make a List of What You Like about Yourself

Go back to my chapter titled "If the Shoe Fits, Wear It," and review the SHAPE section. List the things about the SHAPE God gave you that are good. Don't stop with the first things that come to your mind. Spend some time on this point, and write down at least five positive qualities about yourself.

Step 4: Grow the Gifts God Has Given You

Making the list in step three is just the beginning. Growing in the gifts God has given you is the next step. Beside each thing you like about yourself, write the first action step you will take to develop and grow in that attribute. Know that God will actively work in you to help you grow: "Being confident of this, that he who began a good work in you will carry it on to completion until the day of Christ Jesus" (Philippians 1:6).

Step 5: Make a List of Things You Want to "Throw Out" of Your Inner Closet

Be honest but not brutal. Some people have a hard time seeing their own faults, while others can see little but their faults. This is not a time for either extreme. Take an honest, objective look at yourself, but don't tear yourself apart.

Remember that most of the junk in our closets is not the huge things, but little stuff that just piles up—stuff like jealousy, greed, selfishness, bitterness, and pride. I was convicted as I read in Matthew 23:25–26, where Jesus says to the Pharisees, "You hypocrites! You clean the outside of the cup and dish, but inside they are full of greed and self-indulgence. . . . First clean the inside of the cup and dish, and then the outside also will be clean." We've got to take the time to work on our hearts from the inside out.

Step 6: Take Action

Beside each "throw-away" item, write the first action step you will take toward change. For me, people pleasing was something that took up way too much space in my closet. Being a people pleaser was on my throw-away list. I'm learning that it's OK to say no to some things. I don't have to be on every committee or sign-up sheet that goes around. If someone is disappointed in me for declining a certain activity, I just have to know that I've prayed about what I'm to be involved in.

As we make commitments to change and decide on action steps, it is comforting to remember how very gracious and forgiving God is toward all the junk in our lives: "He does not treat us as our sins deserve or repay us according to our iniquities. For as high as the heavens are above the earth, so great is his love for those who fear him; as far as the east is from the west, so far has he removed our transgressions from us" (Psalm 103:10–12). And Isaiah 30:19 says, "How gracious he will be when you cry for help! As soon as he hears, he will answer you."

Step 7: Circle Items That Require Extra Help

Circle any items on your "throw-away" list that you don't think you can throw away by yourself. As we discussed in my second chapter, "Dirty Laundry," there are times when professional help is required. If you're having a hard time taking that step and getting help, take your fears and hesitations to God in prayer. Ask Him for guidance and wisdom.

There are certain things in our lives that, although we know they are bad for us, we have a hard time letting go of. Even things that are bad for us can, in some way, make us feel comfortable or secure. But as we grow in our relationship with the Savior, we have to let go of the harmful things that linger in the dark corners of our lives. Bringing the light of outside help into the dark can be an adjustment, especially if it is a sudden bright light. But God has chosen you as His royal princess, and he has called you out of darkness and into his light. "You are a chosen people, a royal priesthood, a holy nation, a people belonging to God, that you may declare the praises of him who called you out of darkness into his wonderful light" (1 Peter 2:9).

Bring in the New

No matter what we have in our past—and I mean no matter *what*!—God's unfailing love allows us to start fresh and new: "The unfailing love of the LORD never ends! By his mercies we have been kept from complete destruction. Great is his faithfulness; his mercies begin afresh each day" (Lamentations 3:22–23 NLT). And

with God's new mercies come the opportunity to be a brand-new person: "Therefore, if anyone is in Christ, he is a new creation; the old has gone, the new has come!" (2 Corinthians 5:17).

Becoming new is a process! When we ask God to change us in ways that please Him, He will do good and wonderful things. He will put new things in our lives every day: "love, joy, peace, patience, kindness, goodness, faithfulness, gentleness, and self-control"—the fruit of the Holy Spirit who lives in us (Galatians 5:22–23). These are the things that begin to make our SHAPE complete. The God "who began a good work in you will carry it on to completion until the day of Christ Jesus" (Philippians 1:6).

Here's the catch: if we truly want to have the closet of our hearts designed by the great Creator, Organizer, and Finisher, we must spend time with Him. Now that you've made this great start, stay in touch with God on a regular basis. It's that day-to-day cleanup that keeps us from getting back to the same old clutter. Why wait until you need another overhaul? Give Him a chance every day to show you where things should be put to make the most of your design.

You have the *best* Designer in the world. Trust Him! He will make all the difference.

Extreme Makeover

Opening Scripture: Pray that God would speak to you in a specific way today as you study His Word. Then read Romans 8:29.

Head-to-Toe Makeover: Have you ever watched one of those makeover shows? You know, the ones where someone gets new teeth, new hair, cosmetic surgery, and a whole new wardrobe. You wouldn't even recognize these people if you were only shown "before" and "after" photos. Some of these makeovers give new meaning to the word *extreme*. Maybe when you watch shows like that, you think of all the things you would change about yourself. If you could, maybe you would change your nose or the color of your hair. If given the chance, most females would love a makeover. It's fun to get a new look and go from "before" to "after."

What do you think? Why do you think our culture is so infatuated with makeovers? ____

____

If you could get one part of you "made over," what would it be? ____

____

Did you know that God is in the extreme makeover business? He sees and loves the "before" you, but He has a great plan for the "after" you. He sees what you can become; and when you rely on Him, He can re-make you with the ultimate extreme makeover.

Fill in the blanks: Reread Romans 8:29 and fill in the missing words.

"For those God ___________ he also predestined to be ___________ to the ______________ of his _____, that he might be the ______________ among many brothers."

Think about it: God's end goal for what He wants you to be like isn't Jennifer Aniston, Hilary Duff, or even Billy Graham. Those goals are way to small. He wants you to be like His Son, Jesus Christ. He wants you to act like Him, love like Him, think like Him, and talk like Him. He wants you to be changed from the inside out.

☆ **A Good, Long Look in the Mirror:** Have you ever considered how many hours a week you spend in front of a mirror? If you're like most girls, you spend at least an hour or more looking in the mirror each day. There's the time when we dry our hair, pluck our eyebrows, and apply makeup. We stand in front of the mirror to style our hair and to evaluate our outfits. While there's nothing wrong with looking nice, it's important to remember that what's on the outside isn't the real us. It's just the shell the real us wears to live on the earth. So what mirror will the real me, not the shell I live in, look in?

What does the Word say? Read James 1:22–25. In this passage the Bible is compared to a mirror. According to verse 25, those who look at it intently gain what?

- ❑ Riches
- ❑ Freedom

- ❑ Fame
- ❑ Biblical knowledge

Reread verse 25. What does this verse promise will happen when we obey God's Word? ______________________________

____

Think about it: God's Word is the mirror for our spiritual life. When we look into it by reading, studying, and memorizing, we can see what God sees when He looks at us. God uses the Word to show us areas where we are doing well and others we need to change.

What's your experience? Describe a situation where God used a Bible verse or passage to show you something that He wanted you to change. ______________________________

____

____

____

Has there been a time when God used His Word to encourage you that you were on the right track? If so, describe that situation. ____

____

____

☆ **Change—From the Inside Out:** The problem with makeover shows is that they only focus on the outside person. No one ever talks about the real identity of the one they are making over. That's the difference between a God makeover and one that the world offers. God wants to makeover the real you. He's interested in way more than the color of your hair or the shape of your eyebrows. He wants you to change from the inside out.

What does the Word say? Read Matthew 23:25–26. What do these verses teach about only taking care of our outer appearance and neglecting our hearts? ____

____

____

What do you think? Why do you think God is more interested in the inside of a person than the outside? ________________________

____

____

Are you more interested in your outer appearance or the condition of your heart? Explain your answer. ________________________

____

____

____

☆ **The Road to Change:** All of us have areas where we are growing and doing well. And we all have parts of our lives where we need God to radically change us. What are the steps to participating with God in His makeover process?

1. Prayer. If we're going to change, prayer is the first step. We need to humbly come before God, asking Him where He wants to change us.

Ask Him to show you where you are more like the world than Him.

Fill in the blanks: Read Psalm 139:23–24 and fill in the missing words. "__________ me, O God, and ________ my __________; ________ me and know my anxious ____________. See if there is any _____________ way in me, and lead me in the ________ everlasting."

Pray about it: You may want to pray this verse back to God when you start your quiet time each day. You can trust that if you ask Him to search your heart, He will. He will show you places in you that need to change. Instead of jealousy, He wants to form in you a generous and giving heart. Instead of pride, humility. Instead of selfishness, selflessness. Ask Him to reveal the places in your heart that need a makeover, and be prepared: He will answer you.

2. Renew your mind. Since change comes from the inside out, it's crucial that your mind changes. What we think about determines what we'll become.

What do you think? How much "mind time" do you give to the things of God? ____

What does the Word say? Read Romans 12:2. What is the key to being transformed (changed)? ______________________________________

____

____

We renew our minds when we spend time looking in the Word of

God, our spiritual mirror. The more we know the Word, the more our thoughts and hearts will look like Him. The more the inside changes, the more the outside will change too.

✔ **Try This:** We renew our minds when we read, study, or memorize Scripture. What practical steps will you take to renew your mind this week? ____

____

____

Is there an activity that has a worldly influence on you that you need to replace with an activity that has a godly influence? If so, what is your action plan for change? ______________________________

____

____

✞ **Living the Word:** Becoming conformed to the image of Jesus is a lifelong process. No one ever gets 100 percent there. But each day, as we determine to become less like the world and cooperate with Him, we'll become more like Jesus.

Read Philippians 1:6.

- Who is the "He" referred to in this verse? ____________________
- What promise do we find in Philippians 1:6? __________________

____

____

• God promises to continue His makeover on you for the rest of your life. Aren't you thankful that He doesn't just leave us the way we are? Take a few moments to write a prayer thanking Him that He is working in you to make you more like His Son, Jesus.

____

____

____

____

____

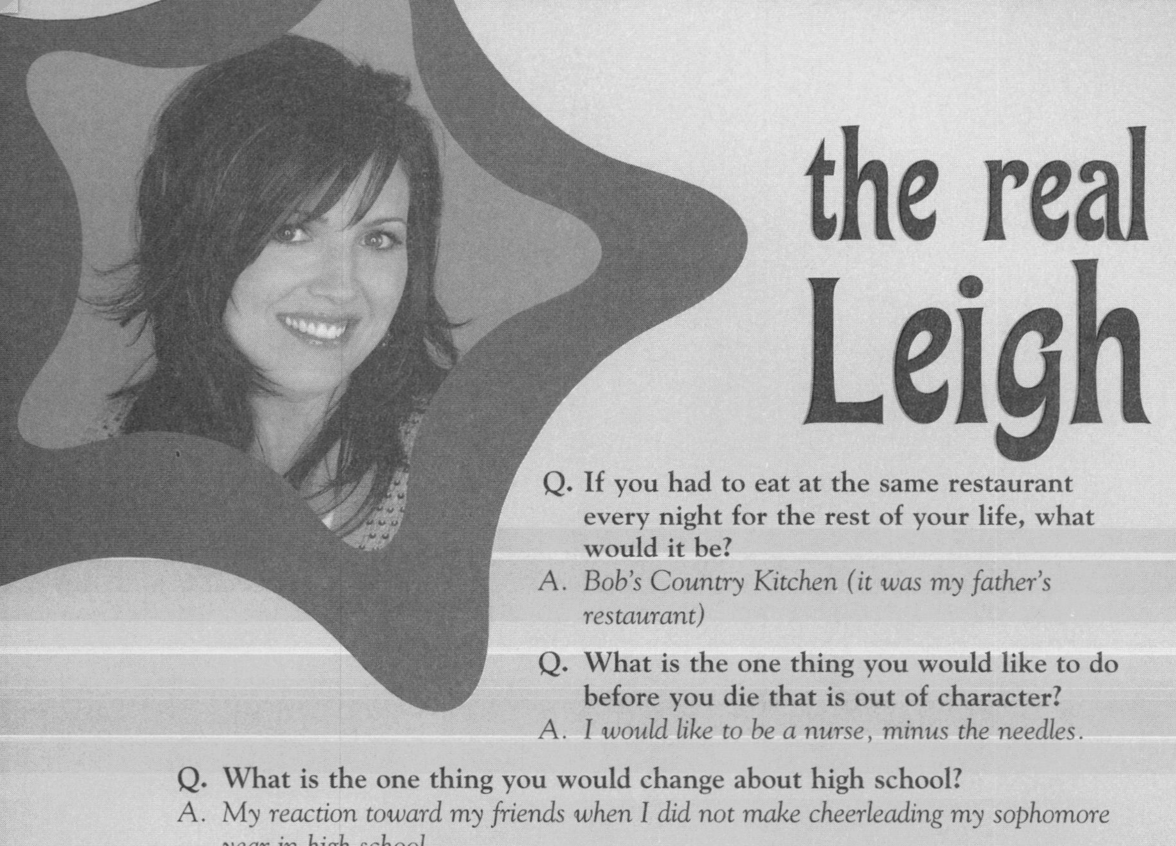

the real Leigh

Q. If you had to eat at the same restaurant every night for the rest of your life, what would it be?
A. *Bob's Country Kitchen (it was my father's restaurant)*

Q. What is the one thing you would like to do before you die that is out of character?
A. *I would like to be a nurse, minus the needles.*

Q. What is the one thing you would change about high school?
A. *My reaction toward my friends when I did not make cheerleading my sophomore year in high school.*

Q. What is the one material possession you would take from Denise?
A. *Her platinum diamond ring given by Word Records for Point of Grace's first platinum-selling record.*

Q. What characteristic do you love most about yourself?
A. *I have skinny legs.*

Q. What is the most embarrassing thing about yourself?
A. *I have a habit of belching in or out of public.*

Q. What is the one thing you tried out for and never made?
A. *I tried out for cheerleading my sophmore year in high school and did not make it. I was completely devastated!!*

the games girls play

A coach is one
who has gone before us—
someone who can
show us the way.

Without wise leadership, a nation falls;
with many counselors, there is safety.
Proverbs 11:14 NLT

Choosing a Great Coach

Life is kind of like a game, isn't it? In life we experience wins and losses. We learn the importance of teamwork and playing by the rules. And just like in a game of basketball or soccer, we find that if we want to win at the game of life, we can't just wait for the game to happen to us. We have to take control and be on the offensive. We have to develop game plans and make deliberate choices if we want to win.

In my three chapters, I want to talk with you about some of the choices you can make as you play the game of life. The first choice we'll talk about is who your coach will be. If you're on a sports team, you probably didn't get to choose your coach; but in the game of life, you get to choose. You don't have to settle for whoever life throws your way.

Why do you even need a coach? Why can't you just play this game of life on your own? Well, I suppose you could. And since we're talking about choices, I have to say, that whether or not to choose a life coach is up to you. But there are so many blessings to having someone older and wiser walk beside you and speak truth into your life as you make this sometimes-difficult journey. Let me share with you some of the reasons you might choose to have a coach/mentor as you live out the game of life.

Reasons to Choose a Coach

First, the Bible teaches the importance of listening to and learning from others. In Titus 2:4 Paul tells the older women to "train the younger women." The book of Proverbs also talks about the value of listening to the advice of others: "Listen to advice and accept instruction, and in the end you will be wise" (19:20), and "Without advice plans go wrong, but with many advisers they succeed" (15:22 GW). Throughout the Bible we are given example after example of how people, through their relationships with others, were taught, encouraged, and cautioned. The apostle Paul loved Timothy and delighted in teaching and "coaching" him. Mary's cousin Elizabeth brought her much comfort. And Ruth cherished and received all that Naomi, her mother-in-law, had to say. Ruth actually *appreciated* her advice. (How many of us appreciate the advice of others?)

Second, since older people have had more life experiences, they have wisdom that they have gained along the way—wisdom that can help you in what you are experiencing now. The game of life can put some pretty tough obstacles in our path, and the wisdom of someone who's been through a similar experience can help us make it through.

Choosing a Great Coach

A coach is one who has gone before us—someone who can show us the way. I was the baby in my family, and I would get so mad at my older sisters because they got to do things long before I did—like wearing makeup, dating, driving the car, and even sitting at the adult table for Thanksgiving dinner. But now as I look back on those memories, I realize that watching them go first provided an opportunity for me to learn from their experiences.

I was in my late twenties before I understood the value of a mentor. Now I am *passionate* about this topic, because I've seen what a blessing a mentor has been for my life. I want you to have the same blessings.

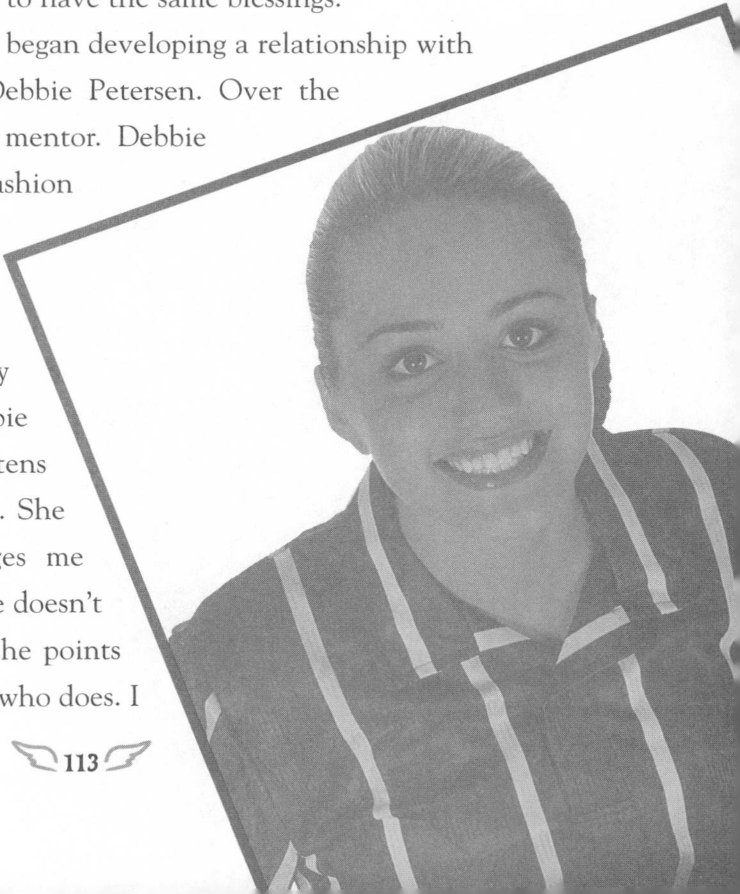

When I was twenty-seven, I began developing a relationship with a wonderful woman named Debbie Petersen. Over the years Debbie has become my mentor. Debbie and I discuss everything from fashion to forgiveness. She provides me a safe haven where I can be completely honest. I feel no hesitation at all in admitting my deepest feelings to her. Debbie does not judge me, but she listens to me with unconditional love. She prays with me and encourages me when life's challenges arise. She doesn't always have the answers, but she points me in the direction of the One who does. I can always count on her responses to be grounded with a godly perspective. I have found that receiving instruction and counsel in a loving manner from Debbie has made me a better person.

Qualities of a Coach Worth Following

But you can't let just anyone be your coach. You have to take the initiative and be in control. You have to be on the offensive and choose the right coach for your life. Here are some things you should look for in a coach.

A Great Coach Has a Plan of Action

Have you ever heard the saying "If you fail to plan, you plan to fail"? Your plan determines your destination—you can take that to the bank! My first vocal coach was a man named Mr. Rogers. Not the Mr. Rogers from PBS children's television, but a very sweet man all the same. Mr. Rogers's plan of action was to teach me how to sing correctly. The most difficult part in his plan was the fact that I had to *practice*! I have a friend whose prayer for wisdom was how I felt about practice: "Lord, help me to go to sleep and wake up wise, because I don't want to do the hard work!" Wouldn't

it be great if it could happen that way? A great coach knows the importance of a plan of action and knows how to inspire you to do the work necessary to work that plan.

A Great Coach Calls You to Do Your Best

A good coach calls you to do your best even when that means pushing you to do more than you want to do. One particular time while I was in college, I came to a voice lesson so unprepared that my vocal coach asked me to leave and not come back if I wasn't going to take my lessons as seriously as he did. Talk about a cold splash of water in the face! And I needed it! My vocal coach had a passion and a love for teaching. Teaching not only brought him pleasure, he took pride in his students' progress. So when I didn't take his instruction seriously, my coach was insulted—and understandably so.

You know, God wants us to do our best too. In the New Testament, the apostle Paul uses the phrase "more and more" in several places to encourage us to go beyond the good we are already doing and strive for the best: "This is my prayer: that your love may abound *more and more*" (Philippians 1:9). In 1 Thessalonians 4:1, he instructed the Christians in Thessalonica to "live in order to please God," and "to do this *more and more*." Then in 2 Thessalonians, he thanks God for them because their faith was growing "*more and more*" (1:3). When you're looking for a coach for your personal life, look for one who isn't afraid to challenge you to do *more and more*—to do your very best.

A Great Coach Knows the Value of Setting Goals

All through my college years and even before, I had had the dream of being onstage as a member of the group Truth. Years of voice lessons, studying music, and performing weekend after weekend finally paid off. I was three weeks away from graduating college when I was asked to audition. I never would have gotten the opportunity to audition if it hadn't been for the dedicated mentors and teachers who, along the way, had taught me the value of setting goals. Long story short, I was asked to join the group. Wow! I was completely blown away. This had been a goal of mine for six years, and it was finally becoming a reality.

There are some things in life that we *desire* but that are beyond our ability to attain. But *goals* are within our reach. There is a difference in goals and desires. A *goal* is something I want and have some ability to attain. A *desire* is something I want but have no ability to attain.

First Corinthians 15:58 tells us not to "let anyone move you off the foundation of your faith. Always excel in the work you do for the Lord. You know that the hard work you do for the Lord is not pointless" (GW).

Hebrews 12:1–2 urges us to run the race of life by focusing on the goal before us: "Run the race that lies ahead of us and never give up. We must focus on Jesus, the source and goal of our faith" (GW).

A great coach helps you set attainable goals and teaches you how to do the hard work needed to reach them.

Choosing the Right Coach for You

Are you up for the game of your life? Are you ready to begin your search for your life coach? Here are some tips on how to find the right coach for you.

First, You Pray

The first thing you do as you set out trying to choose the right coach for yourself is *pray*. Ask God for wisdom. Ask Him for eyes to see the right person. It may be someone you least expect. Ask Him for guidance and help. Then be patient and give Him time to work.

Qualities to Look For

The first rule of thumb is that your mentor needs to be a *woman*. Relationships with guys are great—as friends, as godly boyfriends, as brothers, fathers, uncles, etc.—but when it comes to choosing a *mentor*, girls of grace need to choose a woman. In a coach-mentor relationship, you share your heart, your hopes, your dreams, your fears. You want to be able to be open and honest—and you want to be able to talk about boys and your feelings about them. There's too much extra "chemistry" going on between a boy and girl to try to have a mentoring relationship with a male. And besides that, no one understands a girl like another *girl*!

Beyond choosing a female, choose someone who is spiritually grounded, trustworthy, respectable, honest, kind, older, and wiser.

Places to Look

OK, now you know what kind of woman to look for, so where do you find such a person? You'll find a quality coach where quality people are. Your church is an excellent place to look for a coach. Look at Sunday school teachers, pastors' wives, or female youth pastors. You also might find a coach in your own family—an aunt, a trusted friend of the family, or even a grandmother. You might find someone at school—a trusted teacher, guidance counselor, or even a sports coach. The point is, hang around places where good things are going on and where good people are hanging out, and your chances of finding a quality coach will greatly increase.

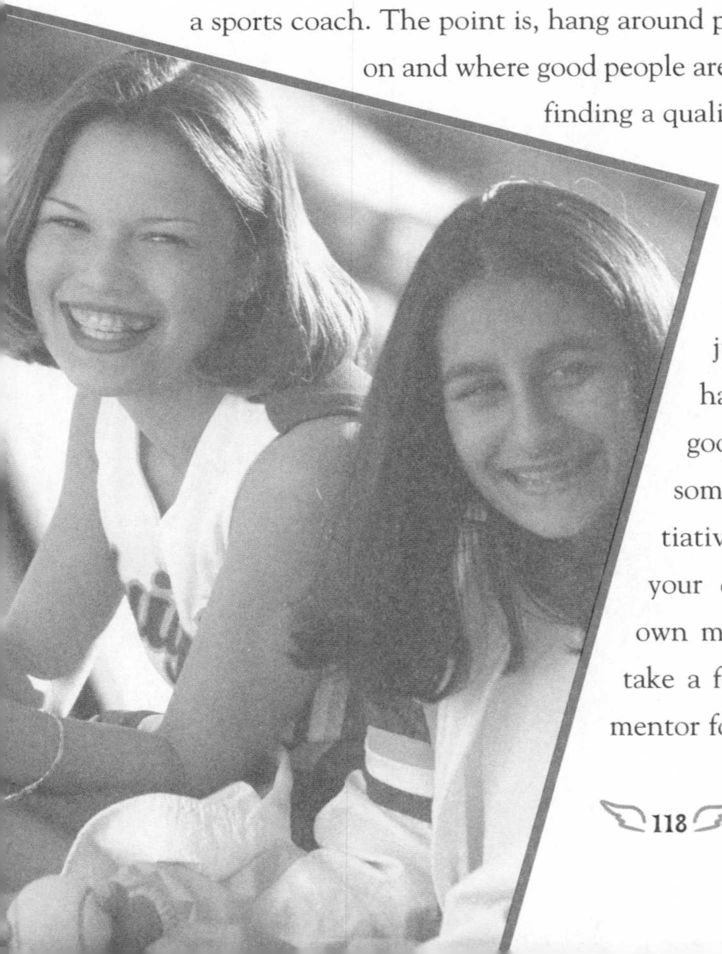

How to Begin a Relationship with Your Coach

Many mentoring relationships just begin naturally because you are hanging out in good places with good people doing good things. But sometimes you have to take some initiative, especially when you are making your own choices and choosing your own mentor. Keep in mind that it may take a few "false starts" to find the right mentor for you. A "false start" is when you start out doing something but things just don't work out at first. False starts are often used as practice for the "real start." So don't be discouraged if your first couple of efforts don't work out.

When you find a woman whom you'd like to get to know a little better, pray some more. If after prayer, you still feel good about pursuing the relationship, ask the woman if you can get together for a few minutes after church or after class. You could get together for a Coke, to pray, to study the Bible, to go shopping, to have lunch, or just to talk.

Find what's comfortable for you, and reach out. Don't be surprised if she's surprised. This may be new to her too. Just be genuine, open, and not pushy. If your first attempt turns out to be a false start, get back on your knees, and pray some more. It's worth the effort!

Of course, the ultimate Coach is Jesus Christ. He loves you more than you can imagine, and He's always ready to begin a relationship with you at any time, anywhere. The choice is yours!

A Life Coach

Opening Scripture: Begin today's study by reading Ruth 1:16. Ask God to speak to you in a specific way as you study His Word.

☆ **What Kind of Coach?** Have you ever had a really great coach? You know, the kind who shows you how to reach down deep inside yourself and do your best? The kind who challenges you when you're slacking and applauds you when you find success? A good coach has a way of really bringing out the best in us. We do better when there is someone on the sidelines who has trained and encouraged us.

Maybe you don't play sports, so you've never had an actual coach. But you may have had coaches in your life who just weren't called coaches. Maybe your coach was a tutor, dance instructor, teacher, parent, or youth leader. Somehow this person always knew what to say to inspire you to do your best.

What's your experience? Who has been the best "coach" in your life? What have you learned from this person? ______________________

____

____

What does the Word say? In Ruth 1:16, Ruth is talking to the coach in her life, her mother-in-law, Naomi. After Ruth found herself a widow at a young age, she realized that she was going to need someone to help her and teach her.

A Life Coach

Reread Ruth 1:16. How serious is Ruth about following Naomi?

- ❑ She's totally kidding.
- ❑ She is very committed.
- ❑ She's not at all serious.
- ❑ She'll follow if it's convenient.

What do you think? Ruth found a coach and decided to pursue that relationship with all that she had. What about you? Have you ever found someone older than you who could coach you in your spiritual walk? If so, who is that person? ______________________________

Think about it: While it's important to have many older, wiser people in our lives, it's essential to find one person in particular who can encourage us in our spiritual walks. This may be a youth leader or older woman who goes to your church. You'll want your primary coach to be a female, as she can understand more of what you're dealing with. Make sure that she has a strong walk with Jesus Christ. Is she someone you want to become like someday? Does she honor Christ in her choices? Is she someone your parents approve of?

✩ The Difference a Coach Makes

What does the Word say? Read Proverbs 19:20 and fill in the missing words.

"__________ to advice and __________ instruction, and in the end you will be ______."

Did you catch it? When we listen to the coaches in our lives, what will the end result be? ______________________________

What's your experience? Has there ever been a time in your life when you listened to a coach and were wiser because of it? Describe the situation.

____

____

What do you think? Read Hebrews 10:24–25. In what practical ways do you think having a coach could encourage you? ______________

____

____

What does the Word say? Read Hebrews 3:13. What benefits does encouragement to one another bring?

- ❑ It makes us run a marathon.
- ❑ It keeps us from the consequences of sin.
- ❑ It makes us happy.
- ❑ There is no benefit.

God never intended for Christians to "go it alone." We all need people in our lives who help and support us as we follow after Him. The more people you have in your life who encourage you to pursue Him, the easier it will be to do so.

☆ **Finding Your Life Coach:** Maybe you're thinking that you just don't know anyone who walks with Christ and would be willing to invest in your life. Well, don't be discouraged. Remember that God wants you to grow and that He is capable of sending someone to help that happen. There may be someone in your life already who you have just overlooked. Maybe you have an older relative who would be your coach. Or you could ask a youth leader from your church if she would be willing to do so.

Pray about it: Start praying daily that God would bring you a lady to coach you in your spiritual walk. Keep your eyes open to whom He will bring. It may be someone you would have never expected.

Think about it: The best way to meet others who are following Christ is by going where those people hang out. If you are looking for a godly coach but you rarely attend church, you'll find that it is hard to meet one. Make sure you are putting yourself in positions where you can meet godly role models, and you'll be surprised at how many will just "pop" into your life.

What's your experience? Do you have a role model in your life who wholeheartedly supports your decision to walk with Christ? If so, who?

____

____

If you do, you may want to ask this person to be your coach. If not, keep praying and waiting. God will bring you someone in His timing. You may wonder what you will do once you and your coach agree to meet. First of all, get to know each other. You'll want to share a little bit about what you hope to get out of the relationship. Determine a time and place to meet, and decide what you'll do during that time. Maybe you'll study a book of the Bible or read and discuss a Christian book. Or you could just meet and discuss what God is teaching you both. Whatever you do during that time, you'll want to pray together. If you feel uncomfortable praying at first, just ask your coach to pray aloud, and you can pray silently.

✔ **Try This:** Read Philippians 2:1–2. Take a few minutes to write this verse somewhere you will see it each day. You may want to attach a sticky note to your computer screen or write it on your mirror. When you see the verse, work on committing it to memory. Pray that this verse would describe the relationship that you share with your coach.

✞ **Living the Word:** Reread Philippians 2:1–2.

• Verse 2 can be a good test to see if you and your coach are heading in the right direction. Do these characteristics describe your relationship? Are you like-minded in your decision to follow Christ? Do you have the same love for Him? ______________________________

____

____

• Do you and your coach share the same purpose, to know Christ better? ______________________________________

____

A Life Coach

- If you don't have a coach yet, what practical steps are you going to take to find one? ____

____

- If you do have a coach, you may want to write her a thank-you note today telling her how much you appreciate her. It won't take long, and it will encourage her as she encourages you.

A cheerleader knows
how to find the positive
in the negativity of life
and invites us to
take a new look.

The heartfelt counsel of a friend
is as sweet as perfume.
Proverbs 27:9 NLT

Choosing a Cheerleader

As far back as I can remember, I wanted to be a cheerleader. I think the idea really took hold the year that Santa put pompoms under the Christmas tree. We were your normal, middle-class family, but I had two older sisters—Dana and Reide—and our combined Christmas wish lists were pretty long; so our mom had to be financially creative when it came to choosing gifts for all of us. On one particular Christmas, Mom made all three girls a set of pompoms. One set was red and white, another was green and white, and the third was green and yellow. I got the green and yellow set. *I loved them*! I was so excited and thrilled as I pretended to be a cheerleader.

From that early age, I've always valued the role of cheerleaders at any sporting event, and I've learned to value them in my personal life as well.

The chief role of a cheerleader is that of *encourager*.

A Cheerleader "Cheers" You On!

We all need a cheerleader as we play the game of life, because we all need encouragement from time to time. Life can be hard, and we need someone who can cheer us on and pick us up when we fall down. We need someone who can encourage us when we feel defeated. A cheerleader knows how to find the positive in the negativity of life and invites us to take a new look.

Barnabas, in Acts 9:26–15:39, was the apostle Paul's personal cheerleader. In fact, Barnabas's name means "son of encouragement"! After Paul's sudden conversion from being a killer of Christians to being a follower of Christ, the Christians in Jerusalem were afraid of him and wouldn't have anything to do with him—and understandably so. But Barnabas believed in Paul, took him around to the other believers, and convinced them to take him in. Barnabas's willingness to stand beside Paul resulted in a long-lasting, trusting relationship between the two men. Barnabas was a great help to Paul in his service and in teaching of the gospel. And the rest is history—or, shall I say, the New Testament!

I, too, have had great encouragers in my life. One of those was my mom. One night when I was twelve years old, as my mother was driving us home after Wednesday night church service, we were talking about my singing abilities. The way I remember it, Mom simply said, "Leigh, you have a very special gift!" That's it. That's all she said. I don't recall the drive home, going to bed that night, or even the next morning; but I have *never* forgotten those words. My mom probably doesn't remember saying them, but her words encouraged me to stay in the game. Her "pompoms" weren't green and yellow like mine; they were the colors of encouragement and enthusiasm.

I've already introduced you to another very special cheerleader in my life—my friend and mentor, Debbie Peterson. There are not enough trees in the forest to write all I have learned from her and her experiences. Talk about an encourager! She refuses to let me feel defeated. I love being around her. I hang on her every word; her wisdom infuses me! Debbie has an incredible testimony of God's redeeming love and mercy and is enthusiastic about sharing it with others. I look at her life and want to be more like her: she studies the Bible, is a prayer warrior, and takes time to invest in people's lives. Debbie understands her frailty as a human being and that without Christ she is nothing. Understanding that, she has a heart of compassion and not condemnation, which is her most beautiful characteristic. Debbie's very life encourages me to live better.

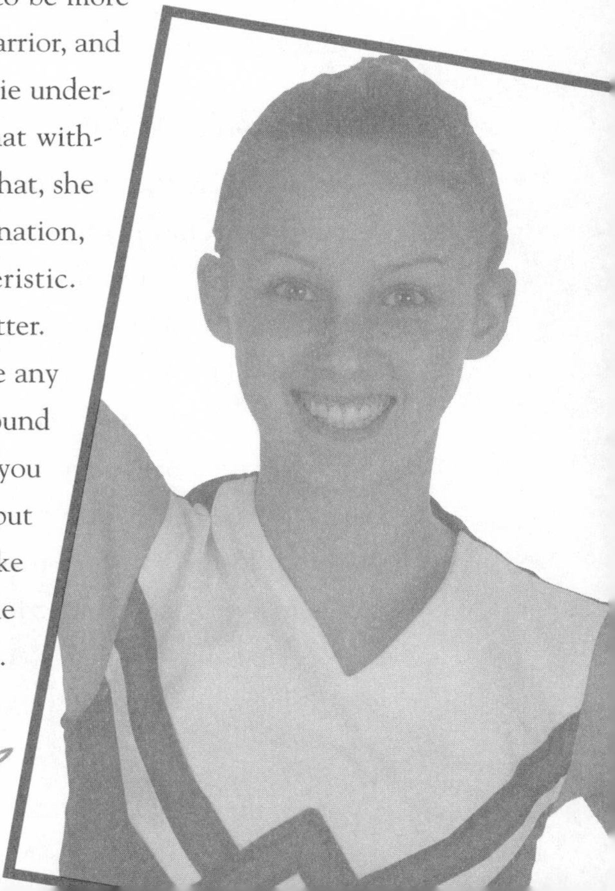

Think about the people in your life. Are any of them cheerleaders? Or do you hang around with people who discourage you and bring you down? Some of the people in our lives are put there by God for very specific purposes—like Barnabas was put into Paul's life to enable him to share the gospel with the world. Others, like my mom, are put into our lives by birth. We really have no choice about our parents, our brothers and sisters, and aunts and uncles. I was very blessed to have an encouraging mom, but not everyone is. But we do have a choice concerning many of the other people who are in our lives, like my friend Debbie.

Be a Cheerleader to Attract Cheerleader Friends

You've probably been told that the best way to find a friend is to be a friend. Well, the best way to find a cheerleader for your life is to be a cheerleader in the lives of others. Several verses in the Bible talk about encouragement, and these verses give us great insight into what makes a cheerleader-friend:

A Cheerleader Builds Up Others

"Encourage one another and build each other up" (1 Thessalonians 5:11).

To build someone up is the opposite of tearing her down or destroying her. Think about your conversations and the conversations of your friends. Do your words and actions tear people down, or do they build them up? How about the people around you? Do their words and actions make you feel like you are being taken apart brick by brick, or do they build you up and make you stronger and more complete? Depending on your answer, it may be time to make some new choices.

Nothing pleases God more than when you choose to please Him. If you ask for His help in making changes in your heart, behavior, speech—anything in your life—He will work with you. The changes won't happen overnight; but stick with Him, and He will work wonders in you.

And if you need to choose some new friends, bring this to God, too, and let Him help you with that. Sometimes you need to leave old friends behind completely, and sometimes you just need to add new friends, while keeping the old.

A Cheerleader Encourages Outbursts of Love and Good Deeds

"Think of ways to encourage one another to outbursts of love and good deeds" (Hebrews 10:24 NLT).

Wow! What a cool way to say that. I want to have "outbursts" of love and good deeds in my life. That sounds fun! When you're with your friends, what kind of behavior and words "burst" out of you? Are they motivated by love? Do they result in good deeds? If not, think about the choices you can make to become a better cheerleader and to choose the kinds of friends who will cheer you on to this kind of outburst.

A Cheerleader Assures Us of God's Grace—No Matter What!

"My purpose in writing is to encourage you and assure you that the grace of God is with you no matter what happens" (1 Peter 5:12 NLT).

I don't know a single person who doesn't need this assurance. I blow it daily, and daily I need to be assured of God's grace. I need to be reminded that He loves me—*no matter what*! Think about the "no matter whats" in your life. You know what I'm talking about. The words you said. The lie you told. The thing you did. The secret you are holding inside. You need a cheerleader in your life who will assure you that the grace of God is with you no matter what.

And you need to be the kind of cheerleader who assures other people the same.

Now, please don't get me wrong. This does not mean that God is OK with the wrong you did or that there won't be any consequences for our sin. God is *not* OK with our sin, and the consequences are real. But Jesus has paid the price, and as 1 John 1:7 says, "If we are living in the light of God's presence, just as Christ is, then we have fellowship with each other, and the blood of Jesus, his Son, cleanses us from every sin" (NLT).

But even more than the "no matter whats" that we do, this verse is talking about the "no matter whats" that happen to us. The people Peter was writing to were undergoing severe persecution, and Peter was assuring them that "no matter what" happened to them, they were not alone. God was with them, and His grace surrounded them. So no matter what happens to you, God is right beside you. He doesn't always take the pain away, but He cries with you.

Are you the kind of cheerleader friend who encourages others to look to God's grace when the "no matter whats" of life start pressing in? Do you have cheerleader friends who help you do the same? If you don't have those kinds of friends, the choice is up to you. Remember, be that kind of friend, and you will attract that kind of friend.

A Cheerleader Encourages Obedience to God's Teaching

"Teach these truths, Timothy, and encourage everyone to obey them" (1 Timothy 6:2 NLT).

Obey is not a popular word. In fact, breaking the rules and doing it your own way are much more popular today. But the best of friends hold the line when it comes to doing it God's way.

The thing about God's commands is that they are for our *good*. Why do you think God has told us (in no uncertain terms) that sex outside of marriage is wrong? It's not because He doesn't want us to have any fun, but because He has created us so that we long for the loving, committed relationship that only marriage can bring. Sex is the precious fragrance that gives marriage its sweetness. When we play with sex before the right time and in the wrong relationship, we spoil what God meant to be beautiful and special. And when married people break their promise to each other by having sex with someone outside their marriage, they bring so much hurt to themselves, their spouse, and to their children. All of this and much more are behind God's commands to keep sex inside of marriage. What I want you to see here is that all of God's rules and commands are for our good and benefit. They are not arbitrary.

A good cheerleader friend will encourage you to obey God's teachings, even when those teachings are hard, because she knows this is best for you.

And as you grow into this kind of cheerleader friend, you, too, will encourage others to obey God's truths.

These are just a few of the characteristics of a great cheerleader friend, but they'll get you started in your search for friends who will cheer you on and as you strive to become that kind of friend yourself!

The Gift of You!

I find it hard to believe that you were created just to go to school, play, shop, and then die. No, you were created for greater things. Among other things, you were created to bless others, and what greater blessing could you share than the blessing of yourself? Someone once said that we need three things each day: someone to love, something to do, and something to look forward to. As you give yourself to others as a cheerleader friend, besides blessing them, you will be fulfilling these three needs in yourself: you will be loving others, you will be doing good for others, and your days will be filled with purpose and be worth looking forward to.

With Jesus by your side as the perfect cheerleader, you can become a lifelong encourager of others. Are you ready to be a cheerleader friend? Are you prepared to make the choices needed to bring some cheerleader friends into your life? If your answer to these questions is yes, then get your pompoms, and let's go!

STUDY GUIDE

Someone on the Sidelines

Opening Scripture: Read 1 Thessalonians 5:11. Ask God to speak to you in a specific way as you study His Word today.

Someone Calling Out Your Name: Have you ever played on a team or taken part in a competition? If so, you know that one of the first things you do when you get on the field or the court is look for your "fans." Now, you aren't Tiger Woods, so you probably don't have a whole crowd watching your every move. But chances are, someone is in the stands there to watch you. It may be your mom or dad or even your best friend. That person sees when you score and even when you blow it! And every now and then, you may hear her call out your name above the crowd! "Go, Mary!" "Good job, Sue!" It's those cheers that give you the strength to push on through the last play. You know someone is rooting for you and watching your every victory, no matter how small.

What's your experience? Have you ever had the experience where someone you love came to watch you compete or perform? If so, how did it make you feel?______________________________________

____

____

Maybe you have never had someone come to watch you. If so, how did you feel? ____

____

____

What does the Word say? Reread 1 Thessalonians 5:11. How can you be a cheerleader in someone else's life and build them up?____________

____

____

What do you think? Why is it so important that we cheer for those whom God has put in our lives? ______________________________

____

____

☆ **Finding a Cheerleader:** Maybe you can't think of a single person in your life who cheers you on. Maybe you feel so alone and that no one really cares about you. If so, remember that your ultimate cheerleader is God. He is there with you every second of every day. He watches you sleep, gives you each breath, and cares more for you than you even care about yourself. He is for you! He loves you beyond what you could ever dream. Ask Him to help you find a cheerleader, or several cheerleaders, who can physically express the love and care that He has for you.

Pray about it: Ask God to bring you a cheerleader to cheer for you. Pray that He would provide you with a friend or family member who will encourage you as you follow God. Now, be open to how He answers this prayer. Sometimes His answers don't look like what we think they will. They may not be who we thought they would be or come from the obvious places we would look, but God will answer your prayer. Be patient and open to His answer.

Think about it: One of the best ways to find a cheerleader is to be one. Who do you know who needs encouragement? Maybe there is someone in a class or in your family who needs to hear an uplifting word from you. Make sure that you take the opportunity to build this person up. You will not only help her, you will find that you are making a friend as well.

What does the Word say? Read Romans 15:1–2. What does this passage teach that our focus should be?

- ❑ Finding cheerleaders to encourage us
- ❑ Building other people up
- ❑ Having a lot of friends
- ❑ Telling others how to change

It's one of the ironies of life that when we focus on serving others, we find that our own needs are often met. When you look for others to encourage, you don't really have to look for those to encourage you. More than likely, they will just show up in your life.

What's your experience? Has there ever been a time when you made it a point to meet someone else's need and found out that you were encouraged in the process? If so, describe what happened. __________

____

____

____

✭ Cheering with a Purpose

Fill in the blanks: Read 1 Samuel 23:16 and fill in the missing words.

"And Saul's son Jonathan went to __________ at Horesh and __________ him find __________________ in God."

When we are looking for cheerleaders or wanting to be one in someone else's life, we need to remember that the purpose isn't just to make someone feel good. The purpose of a cheerleader is to point someone else to God.

What does the Word say? Reread 1 Samuel 23:16. What did Jonathan, David's cheerleader, do for him?______________________________

____

____

What does it mean? What are some practical ways we can do that for someone we are trying to encourage?____________________________

____

____

When you want to help someone else find strength in a tough time, it's important to point that person to God's character and His Word.

What do you think? When we encourage someone to remember God's character, we're reminding him or her of who God is and what He is like. How would this help someone going through a tough time?

____

____

What's your experience? God's Word is the ultimate pompom when encouraging others. Has there ever been a time when someone gave you a Bible verse that changed your perspective when you were having a hard time? If so, describe the situation. __________________

____

____

____

____

✔ **Try This:** Read Hebrews 10:24. Have you ever really stopped to think about the influence you have with your friends? You can encourage them to do or say things just by your very presence in their lives. You can set an example in your family with your siblings and even your parents. The verse says you can spur someone else to do the right thing. By your example you can start a ripple effect of encouragement that can change your family, your school, your town, or your world.

Take some time to do just what this verse suggests: consider. Make a list of some ways that you can start a chain reaction of encouragement in your family. How can you cheer on others in your school?

Don't be afraid to dream big! I know of someone who wrote a different Bible verse on the back window of his car each morning before school. Each person who saw him driving to school was encouraged by God's Word and reminded of God's love. That was fifteen years ago, and people I know still talk about it. You never know what effects your choices to encourage will have. ____________________

____

____

✝ **Living the Word:** Read Philippians 2:3–5.

• Encouragement is less an action and more a lifestyle. In what ways can you daily consider others better than you? ____________________

____

____

• What do you think verse 3 means by "selfish ambition"? What are some ways to overcome acting this way? ____________________

____

____

• It just comes naturally to look out for our own interests. Make a list of several people in your life, then next to each name write one way you can focus on his or her interests.____________________

____

____

____

• Verse 5 sums up the definition of an encourager. Write out a prayer asking God to help you daily choose the attitude of Jesus. Ask Him to give you the strength to model His love and care for people.________

____

____

____

____

____

____

____

The wise referee
knows that her actions
should complement her authority,
not contradict it.

Hold on to instruction, do not let it go;
guard it well, for it is your life.
Proverbs 4:13

Choosing to Follow a Referee

The colors of a referee's uniform leave no room for confusion. They're black and white with no gray area whatsoever. Interesting, don't you think? Indecision is *not* a quality of a referee.

Although referees are not the most popular people on the field, they are absolutely essential to any sports game—and they are essential to the game of life as well. Like a referee's uniform, the basics of the referee's job are also quite simple:

1. To bring trustworthy wisdom and understanding to the game

2. To enforce the rules and hold players accountable for their actions

3. To provide protective boundaries

In our rational moments, we can see the benefits of having a referee in our lives, but when we want to do something against the rules, we wish we could do away with the referee.

You probably already have several referees in your life: your parents, teachers, youth pastor, and coach. All of these people have been placed in a position of authority and are responsible to bring wisdom, enforce rules, and provide boundaries. You usually don't get to choose who your referees are, but you do get to choose whether or not you follow your referee's lead.

The Benefits of a Good Referee

Let's spend a few minutes thinking about the benefits of a good referee.

A Good Referee Brings Wisdom

Wisdom could be defined as an intelligent attitude toward the experiences of life. Mere *knowledge* is not the same as *wisdom*. Wisdom is knowing how to apply knowledge to make life work. The best kind of referee brings not only firm understanding of the rules of the game but also wisdom that has been gained from years of experience in seeing those rules applied and the game played.

The Bible says, "The LORD gives wisdom, and from his mouth come knowledge and understanding" (Proverbs 2:6) and, "A wise person will listen and continue to learn and an understanding person will gain direction" (Proverbs 1:5 GW). A truly good referee is grounded in God. This is *extremely* important; otherwise, his decisions and counsel will not be reliable.

Have you ever heard the saying "Don't do as I do, do as I say"? While growing up, I only heard it a couple of times at the most, and I never quite understood its meaning until much later. Just recently, I provided an example of this saying without intending to.

One day I was out on our patio deck helping my husband hang a birdhouse on our backyard fence. I had left the glass door open and the screen door pulled to so I could hear and see our two-year-old daughter, Darby Mae. Darby saw me outside and asked, "Mommy, can I go outside too?"

"No, Darby," I answered. "You need to have your shoes on, not just your socks." Darby got surprisingly upset. It took me a minute to realize that I was outside in my socks—without my shoes. What was I teaching her? I immediately apologized.

"Darby Mae, I am so sorry that I told you no. I didn't realize that Mommy was outside in just *her* socks. You can come outside too." Darby Mae came outside, and that was that.

This simple story illustrates an important message: the wise referee knows that her actions should complement her authority, not contradict it. Wisdom comes with experience and practice, and we are blessed when we have referees in our lives who guide us with their wise understanding.

A Good Referee Enforces the Rules

When I was a teenager, I asked my mom if I could go to a party at my friend's house. Mom quickly responded with a firm, "No!" I persisted and pleaded and gave her every reason in the book as to why I should be allowed to go, and I told her how unfair she was being for *not* letting me go. Her final response was, "I am concerned that there will be things going on at that party that frankly, you should not be involved in." Shamefully, I confess that I found a way and went to the party without her permission, only to learn that she was absolutely correct in her assumptions. That party did *not* represent anything good.

Why do we have such a hard time accepting rules that are for our own good? It may have something to do with the fact that we live in a fallen world; and where humanity is, there is sin. This is not an excuse, by any means, to give up the fight. However, it reiterates the importance of having godly people in our lives to hold us accountable for the choices we make.

In reality, it's hard to force other people to do things they don't want to do. But a good referee does enforce the rules by imposing consequences when the rules are broken. Sometimes the referee doesn't have to impose the consequences; sometimes life brings about those consequences naturally. I remember a very painful example that may help you understand that rules are indeed for our benefit.

My sister Reide and I had been warned *not* to ride our motor bike while our parents were not home. One afternoon after school, my sister and I decided to go against that rule. Reide was driving while I was on the back. Well, we hit some gravel and crashed. It was a very nasty fall. Reide's leg was pinned and—we found out later—broken. I was so freaked out; I thought she was going to die. I still have a scar to remind me just how "lucky" we were that it ended in just a broken leg and a very skinned-up elbow. But I can assure you, we learned our lesson. While I didn't like these consequences, they were a firm reminder that there was a price to pay for broken rules.

Of course, there comes a time when a good referee has to step back and let the player make her own choices. I found a poem from an unknown author that reminds us of the limitations of even the best referees. I'll share part of it with you here:

It's Your Move, Daughter

I gave you life,
But I cannot live it for you.
I can teach you things,
But I cannot make you learn.

. . .

I can take you to church,
But I cannot make you believe.
I can teach you right from wrong,
But I can't always decide for you.

. . .

I can advise you about your friends,
But I cannot choose them for you.
I can teach you about sex,
But I cannot keep you pure.
I can tell you the facts of life,
But I can't build your reputation.
I can tell you about drink,
But I can't say NO for you.
I can warn you about drugs,
But I can't prevent you from using them.

. . .

I can teach you about Jesus,
But I cannot make Him your Savior.
I can teach you to obey,
But I cannot make Jesus your Lord.

A Good Referee Provides Protective Boundaries

When Adam and Eve were in the Garden of Eden, God set some very clear and definite boundaries: "The LORD God commanded the man. He said, 'You are free to eat from any tree in the garden. But you must never eat from the tree of the knowledge of good and evil because when you eat from it, you will certainly die' " (Genesis 2:16–17 GW).

The purpose of God's boundary was not to restrict Adam and Eve but to protect them. Adam and Eve had the freedom to obey or disobey God—just as we do. Adam and Eve chose to disobey God, and they lived with the consequences of their choice. Our choices have consequences too. Knowing this up-front should help us make better choices and become more responsible.

The boundaries set up by good referees are for our benefit and protection. When we cross those boundaries, we end up in the danger zone and get into all kinds of trouble. Think of a time when you crossed the boundaries set up to protect you. What were the consequences? You may be thinking of time spent with a boyfriend or at a party. If we are wise, we'll learn from these experiences and choose to stay within God's boundaries next time.

Studies have been done on the behavior of elementary schoolchildren playing on the playground with and without a protective fence. When a fence was in place, the children played freely and happily. They used the whole playground—all the way up to the fence's edge. But when the fence was taken down, they became afraid and insecure and huddled in the center of the playground, staying far from the street, not enjoying the playground equipment. These children understood the benefits and protection offered by boundaries. They didn't see the fence as something that restricted their fun but as something that allowed them the *freedom* to play without fear within their bounds.

This is what God had in mind when He set boundaries in place for us. They are for our protection and safety, so that we can live our lives in freedom and joy within the protection of His bounds.

Choosing a Referee for Your Life

Once again, the choice is yours. God has placed people in your life who bring wisdom, enforce the rules, and provide protective boundaries. And as long as your referees are grounded in God's Word and follow Him, they are worthy of your respect. But I have to offer one word of caution here. Unfortunately, we live in a world where not everyone who sets himself up as an authority figure can be trusted. Just because a person in authority tells you to do something does not mean you should do it. Not everyone who makes and enforces rules is pleasing to God. If you have a "bad referee" in your life who is forcing things on you that you know are wrong, get help from another adult. If the first adult you talk with doesn't help you, keep going until you find someone who will.

Now, with that said, there are many wonderful referees out there who—though not perfect—are to be trusted and followed. This is where the "game of life" becomes even more challenging. *Trust* means taking control out of our own hands and giving it to another person. Just like those children trusted the fence to protect them from the dangers of the street, when you find the right referee, you have to trust that the rules he puts in place are for your good. When your mom or dad says you can't go to a party that they know is bad for you, they are doing it for your good—not to harm you or keep you from having fun. This is where trust comes in. Or if your youth pastor sets up boundaries for a trip the youth group is taking, out of respect and trust, you stay within those boundaries—partly because it's right to obey his authority and partly because you trust his judgment.

Of course, the ultimate referee that every one of us must submit to in our lives is Jesus Christ. He has all the qualities we've talked about here and much more.

Dive into the Game of Life!

As you dive into the game of life, make sure that you have around you the key members of your team. Diligently pursue a coach-mentor to guide and support you. Become an encouraging cheerleader friend so that you can attract such cheerleaders into your own life. And finally, learn the value of a good referee so you can be blessed by the boundaries he or she provides.

As we've said in our other chapters, the best team member you can have is Jesus Christ. When you choose Him as referee, you've chosen one who *always* has your best interests at heart and who *always* sets proper boundaries in place for your good.

So get ready to dive in! Put your feet to the starting line, get your bat in position, get ready for that free throw! The game of life is about to start, and you have been chosen by God to be an eternal winner!

Who Makes the Call?

Opening Scripture: Pray that God would speak to you in a specific way today as you study His Word. Read Romans 13:1–2.

Authority Given by God: Do you remember when you were little and couldn't wait to grow up so no one would tell you what to do anymore? You, like me, may have thought that when you were older you would be your own boss. You would decide when to go to bed, get up, and when to clean your room. It's funny that the older we get, the more "bosses" we seem to have. We have teachers, our supervisor at work, youth leaders and pastors, parents, and even the government. No matter how old we are, there is always going to be someone in authority over us.

Think about it: Why do you think that we have more authority figures over us the older we get? ______________________________

____

____

What do you think? In your own words, define the word *authority*, as you understand it. ______________________________

____

____

What does the Word say? Reread Romans 13:1–2. According to this passage, where does authority come from?

Who Makes the Call?

- ❑ Man has made it up to keep order.
- ❑ God established it.
- ❑ People who want to have no fun dreamed it up.
- ❑ Parents invented it.

When we rebel against our authorities, what does verse 2 say we are really doing? ______________________________

____

What does this passage teach is the result? ______________

____

____

What your experience? Has there ever been a time when you rebelled against authority and suffered consequences for your actions? If so, describe the situation. ______________________

____

____

____

☆ **Obeying Authority Means Obeying God:** When we honor the authorities God has placed in our lives, we are ultimately obeying Him. He's called us to obey those He has placed over us—with the only exception being if they ask us to do something hurtful or that goes against God's Word. We fool ourselves when we think we're obeying God but not honoring those referees He has put in our lives.

Think about it: List the authority figures God has put in your life. You may know some of them personally; and others, like law enforcement officials, you may not. ____________________________________

____

____

What does the Word say? Read Ephesians 6:1–3. What does this passage command regarding our parents? ____________________________

____

____

What promise does God make if we obey our parents?____________

____

____

Think about it: Did you include your parents on your list of authorities? Whether or not you did, they are your main authority in this season of your life. While you did not choose them, it's important to remember that God did. As a matter of fact, we don't get to choose many of our authorities, but we do get to choose our responses to them.

What do you think? If you had to give yourself a grade for how well you obey your parents, how would you score?

- ❑ A—Always obey
- ❑ B—Bad sometimes and good sometimes
- ❑ C—Could seriously improve

❑ D—Don't honor them at all

What's your experience? How well do you obey other authority figures in your life, such as teachers and your boss at work? ____________

____

____

____

☆ **The Benefits of Authority:** Like all of God's gifts to us, He always has a reason. He hasn't put authority in our lives to make us miserable; rather, it is to benefit us. There are three obvious benefits to God-given authority.

1. You gain wisdom from others. Proverbs 13:10 says, "Wisdom is found in those who take advice." When we listen to those who have walked with God longer, we can learn from their experiences. Describe a situation where you learned a lesson from a referee God has put in your life. ________________________________

____

____

____

2. You learn the rules and are taught to follow them. Have you ever tried to play a game that had no rules? If so, how did it work? It probably was a disaster, because in order for a game to be fun for everyone, all players must abide by the rules. It's the same way with life. For cities, families, schools, or even nations to run properly, someone needs to make sure that everyone is playing by the rules. Has there been a time when a referee in your life corrected you because you were disobeying? If so, what good came out of it? ______________________________

____

3. You are protected by boundaries. Referees help us know the boundaries God has set up to protect us. They teach us what is appropriate and what can hurt us. When we obey our authorities, we don't have to worry about suffering consequences for our bad decisions. On the other hand, when we disobey them, we run the risk of getting hurt. What steps can you take to avoid hurtful consequences that result from choices you make? ______________________________

____

____

____

✔ **Try This:** Read Proverbs 19:20. Think of some of the referees God has put in your life. Now write down some ways that you can receive their advice and put it into practice. Maybe you will ask your mom and dad to go for ice cream or a long walk. While you're with them, ask them what they would do in a situation that you're dealing with at school or with a friend. Really listen to what they say. God has placed them in your life for a reason. Do you trust Him enough to obey the calls your referees make? ______________________________

____

____

____

____

✝ **Living the Word:** Read Hebrews 13:17.

• What are we commanded to do in this passage? ___________

____

____

• What responsibility has God given our referees? ___________

____

____

• Have you made the job of your authorities a joy or a burden? Explain your answer. ______________________________

____

____

____

• Are there some changes you need to make in how you respond to the referees God has placed in your life? If so, write them here. ____

____

____

____

____

• Is there a referee you need to ask to forgive you for past behavior? If so, write his or her name here. Make a point to talk with that person today. ______________________________

• When we disobey our authorities, we not only make it hard on them, but we also make it hard on us. Write a prayer asking God to help you be a blessing to those referees He has chosen for you. Remember, when you obey them, you obey Him. ______________

____

____

____

____

____

____

____

the real Heather

Q. If you had to eat at the same restaurant every night for the rest of your life, what would it be?

A. *Cracker Barrel.*

Q. What is the one thing you would like to do before you die that is out of character?

A. *I want to live in a foreign country and learn the native language.*

Q. What is the one thing you would change about high school?

A. *I would not let Lanna Taylor give me highlights the day of prom, because it turned my hair bleach blonde. Believe me, it did NOT look good.*

Q. What is the one material possession you would take from Leigh?

A. *Her Lagos ring (sterling silver diamond emerald cut with gold trim).*

Q. What characteristic do you love most about yourself?

A. *My green eyes. I got them from my mom.*

Q. What is the most embarrassing thing about yourself?

A. *I have to wear a clear Band-Aid on my left earlobe in order to wear an earring because my earlobe is spilt in two (thanks to the heavy earrings in the eighties).*

Q. What is the one thing you tried out for and never made?

A. *I competed in the metropolitan opera competition and did not place!*

me: God's mirror to the world

Being created in the image of God means that we were created to *look* like God—not on the outside, but in our character and in our souls.

God created man in His own image,
in the image of God He created him;
male and female He created them.
Genesis 1:27 NASB

Reflections of a Better Me

"Mirror, mirror, on the wall . . ."

As girls, we've all stood in front of a mirror a time or two. And we all know what a mirror does—it reflects the image of whoever stands before it. Sometimes we like the image we see reflected there, and sometimes we don't. The kind of mirrors we look into reflect our *outside* image. But in my three chapters, I want to talk with you about a different kind of image and a different kind of reflection. The story of our image and our reflection begins . . . in the beginning.

A Different Kind of Creature

"In the beginning, God created . . ." The first chapter of Genesis tells us that God created our whole world. When He created the animals, it says that He created them "after their kind" (vv. 24–25 NASB). But when it came time to create *humans*, we hear a different story. Adam and Eve were not simply created after their kind; they were created "in the image of God" (v. 27 NASB).

But not everyone understands the truth that humans are set apart from the rest of God's creation. I was sad to see this evidenced in one of my daughter's picture books. Ella is an animal lover. When the weather is nice, my husband, Brian, and I take her to the zoo at least once a week. Recently, Brian bought Ella a book about animals. Not only does the book have great information, it also has a lot of colorful pictures! Ella loves for her daddy to read this book to her and show her the pictures of just about every animal you can think of. There is just one thing wrong with the book. The authors evidently believe that humans evolved from some lower animal species, because right in the middle of all the animal pictures is a picture of a human being. Apparently, the authors don't see a significant difference between a human being and an animal.

But as Christians, we know and believe that humans are indeed different from all the other creatures of the world. Let's look at what God said in the Bible: "Let Us make man in Our *image*, according to Our *likeness*" (Genesis 1:26 NASB). Out of all the creatures that God made, only one creature—humankind—was made in the image of God. Being created in the image of God means that we were created to *look* like God—not on the outside, but in our character and in our souls. The fact that human beings are made in the image of God means that we are, in a sense, like God. God created us so that we would reflect His image.

Image Malfunction

Unfortunately, not long after God created the first man and woman, the Bible tells us in Genesis 3 that Adam and Eve sinned against God. Did you catch that? Though they were created to be God's image bearers on earth, Adam and Eve chose disobedience and rebellion instead. Because of their sin, we human beings don't reflect God's image as fully as we did before the Fall. Our moral purity has been lost, and our character does not mirror God's holiness. Our speech no longer continually honors God, and our relationships are often controlled by selfishness rather than love. As commentator Wayne Grudem says, "We are less fully like God than we were before the entrance of sin" through Adam and Eve.[1] That is not a pretty picture, is it?

At this point I know what you may be thinking. *This must be the feel-bad chapter of the book. I picked up this book for what? So Heather can tell me how sinful I am?* Patience, please. Just bear with me. In order to understand and appreciate the good news that's coming, I have to share with you the unfortunate truth about our sin.

This reminds me of two summers ago when Brian, Ella, and I lived nextdoor to an amusement park in Cincinnati, Ohio. Every night at 10:00 p.m., the park would shoot off fireworks. And every night Brian and I would forget they were coming; so when those fireworks exploded, we thought we were being bombed. But think about it: why did the park officials decide to have fireworks at 10:00 p.m. rather than 10:00 a.m.? I'm sure that 10:00 a.m. fireworks would have been easier on those living near the park. But of course, the reason the fireworks were set off at night was that only in the context of a darkened sky could onlookers appreciate the brilliance and grandeur of those beautiful, bright (and loud!) fireworks. In fact, you would have been hard-pressed even to see the fireworks in broad daylight.

In the same way, in order to understand the beauty and glory of God's marvelous grace, we have to see it in the context of the darkened sky of humankind's sinfulness. As writer Anthony Hoekema says, the bad news (or the dark sky) is that even though "fallen human beings still possess the gifts and capacities God has [given us] . . . they now use these gifts in sinful and disobedient ways"—doing things that grieve the heart of God.[2] Rather than fulfilling God's purpose in our lives, we use our abilities, talents, and spiritual gifts to pursue our own selfish agendas. Our God-imaging gifts and abilities were not destroyed by the Fall, but they were perverted. As Hoekema explains, the image of God is still in us, but it is "malfunctioning."[3]

The image of God in us needs to be renewed. And this brings us to the next part of the story—*the good news*!

Image Renewed

Along comes our Knight in shining armor, the Lord Jesus Christ. Jesus is the fireworks in the sin-darkened night. Colossians 1:15 says that He is the "image of the invisible God." Jesus so closely reflects God that He was able to say, "Anyone who has seen me has seen the Father" (John 14:9). Jesus, as the Son of God, is the mirror image of God.

And as the mirror image of God, Jesus solves one of our difficulties as we try to look like God. Our difficulty is this: God is *invisible*. We can't see God, so how can we reflect His image? That's where Jesus comes in. Jesus showed us in living color—in flesh and blood—what God looked like. So if we want to know what God *really* looks like, all we have to do is look at Jesus, the fairest of them all.

When we repent of our sins and trust Jesus as our Savior, we are completely renewed—becoming like Him, reflecting God's image! Before our renewal we used our God-imaging powers in wrong ways, but now we are enabled to use these powers in right ways. That is what Paul meant when he wrote that as Christians we have a new nature that is "being renewed in knowledge in the image of its Creator" (Colossians 3:10).

God's purpose in creating you and me in His image was fulfilled in Jesus Christ. So as we trust in Him, we can be assured that our sins will be forgiven and that our purpose and mission in being God's image bearers will be restored. In fact, it could be said that the goal of our salvation in Christ is to make us more and more like God, or more and more like Christ, who is the perfect image of God (see Romans 8:29). That is what sets us apart from all of God's other creatures; that is what is unique about humankind. And as we become more and more like God, the story of our image becomes clearer as we reflect our Creator.

STUDY GUIDE

Image Overhaul

📖 **Opening Scripture:** Pray that God would speak to you in a specific way today as you study His Word. Read Genesis 1:26–27.

☆ **Created for a Purpose:** Have you ever wondered what on earth you're here for? I mean, you wake up in the morning, go to school, and the next day you do it all over again. Some days are exciting, and some days are just plain hard. At times we can get discouraged and forget that God made us for a reason. The day you were born, all those years ago, was a special day in God's book. He saw you take your first breath and hasn't taken His eyes off you since.

What's your experience? Have you ever felt that you were just a cosmic accident and that God had no purpose for your life? If so, explain how you felt. ____

____

____

What does the Word say? Reread Genesis 1:26–27. In whose image did God create you?

- ❑ Your parents
- ❑ A monkey
- ❑ His own
- ❑ Your own

Image Overhaul

It's pretty amazing that, just as Heather wrote, human beings were created altogether differently than the animals. While He did create your beloved family Fido or Fifi, animals are not created in His image. The Bible says only humans have the divine stamp "in God's image" on them.

Think about it: What does the fact that you were created in the image of God say about your worth? ______________________________

____

____

☆ **Human Rebellion:** The good news is that we were created by God and for God. The bad news is that humanity rebelled against the very Creator who gave them breath. You have probably heard the story about how Adam and Eve disobeyed the one command God gave them in the garden. Because of their choice we have all inherited the same sin nature. Everyone who has ever lived has sinned. The only One who has lived a perfect, sinless life is Jesus Christ.

Fill in the blanks: Read Romans 3:23 and fill in the missing words.

"For _______ have ____________ and fall short of the ____________ of ________."

What does it mean? According to this verse, are you included as one who has fallen short? Explain your answer. ______________________

____

____

____

Rebellion, otherwise known as sin, has a very serious penalty. Romans 6:23 says, "For the wages of sin is death." This is serious news; but luckily, the story doesn't end there. Read on.

☆ **Good News!** The second half of Romans 6:23 says, "But the gift of God is eternal life in Christ Jesus our Lord." God loves us so much He did something about our rebellion. He sent His Son to pay the penalty for our sin so that we could be forgiven and have God's image in us restored.

What does the Word say? Read John 3:16. What is the result for those who receive God's free gift of salvation through Jesus?____________

____

____

What's your experience? Has there ever been a time when you received salvation through faith in Jesus Christ? If so, describe that experience.

____

____

____

If you can't recall a time when you have received this gift and you would like to, pray this prayer. There is nothing magical about the words. God is listening to your heart.

Jesus, thank You for dying on the cross to pay the high price for the sins I have committed. I receive Your gift of salvation and invite you into my heart to be Lord and Savior of my life. Amen.

If you prayed this prayer, be sure that you tell a parent, church leader, or friend who is a Christian. The more support you get, the easier it will be for you to grow in your new relationship with Jesus.

☆ **Growing Means Depending on Him:** For Christians, growing means one thing—depending on His strength in our lives. This doesn't mean that we just sit back and wait on Him to make changes in us. Instead, we cooperate with Him as He changes us from the inside out. Fortunately, He has given us several tools to help us grow.

What does the Word say? Read 2 Peter 1:3–4. According to verse 3, how much of what we need to grow has He given us?

- ❑ Some of what we need
- ❑ Most of what we need
- ❑ None of what we need
- ❑ All of what we need

1. Prayer. As we pray about the different areas in our lives that need change, His power will change us little by little.

2. God's Word. According to verse 4, when we read and apply the promises from His Word, what two results can we expect? ________

____

____

Think about it: Do you take full advantage of prayer and God's Word to help you grow? Explain your answer. ____________________

____

____

____

✔ **Try This:** Read John 3:30. The Christian life is the process of allowing God to become greater in our lives, while we become less. While it sounds simple, it's not at all easy. Take a few moments to make two lists. At the top of one, write the word "decrease." On this list write attitudes or actions that you want to diminish in your life. You may include things like selfishness, jealousy, or lust. Now write "increase" at the top of the second list. On this list include things that you want more of. Examples would be love, patience, or selflessness. Now transfer your list to a note card that you can tuck in your Bible. Pray over your list each day, asking God to help you as you seek for Him to increase and the old you to decrease. ______________

____

____

____

____

____

____

✞ **Living the Word:** Read Colossians 3:10.

• When the Bible talks about "putting on the new self," it doesn't mean putting on a new outfit or even our alter ego. It simply means choosing to act in God's strength instead of our own. When we rely on Him, we find the power to obey.

• What are some practical things you can do to cooperate with God as He changes you from the inside out? ______________________

____

____

____

• Take a few moments to write a prayer thanking God that He doesn't leave you the way you are. Thank Him that He will remake you into His image as you trust and obey Him each day. __________

____

____

____

____

____

____

____

There is no better way
to understand the image of God
than to look at Jesus Christ.

We are children of God, and it has not appeared as yet what we will be. We know that when He appears, we will be like Him, because we will see Him just as He is.
1 John 3:2 NASB

Jesus—The Mirror Image of God

What is it with girls and mirrors? We just can't seem to stay away from them. Have you ever passed by a mirror and not at least glanced in it? Why is that? What are you thinking when you look at yourself in the mirror: *Girl, you're looking good today!* or, *Why did I ever leave the house?* Do you ever look in the mirror and think, *I am the image of God*? I would venture to say that this thought doesn't cross our minds very often—but it should.

In the last chapter, we saw that being created in the image of God is what makes human beings special. It's what sets humanity apart from the rest of God's creation and creatures. So when Ella's animal book says that humans belong to the same classification of animals as monkeys and apes, we know it is wrong because we are gloriously different than monkeys and apes. We, unlike other creatures, have the privilege and high calling of being in the very image of God.

Steaming Up God's Image

However, we also remember that because of humankind's sin, that image has been tarnished and distorted. Think about it this way. What happens to a mirror when you take a shower? It gets clouded over with steam. When you look in a steam-covered mirror, you can vaguely see your image, but the steam makes it difficult. It's frustrating to try to brush your hair when you can't see yourself.

That mirror has one purpose: to reflect your image. Why else does it take up wall space? But now, because of the steam, its ability to function as it was created is minimized. That steam is a picture of what sin does to our ability to image God. We are God's mirrors to the world, but when we are all steamed up with sin, God's image cannot be clearly seen in us.

Yet God has made a way for us to overcome the "steam" of sin. He started by sending His Son to show us what the image of God looks like. Then that perfect image died on the cross for the sins of those who willfully rejected the high calling of being the image of God. Through Jesus's sacrifice, the surface of our "mirror" is wiped clean so that we can, through faith in Christ, fulfill our purpose and beautifully reflect the image of God to the world.

Jesus—The Perfect Image of God

The main focus of this chapter is to look at Jesus as the image of God. As the Bible says, Christ is the "radiance of God's glory and the exact representation of his being" (Hebrews 1:3). The "radiance" that Christ gives off is not His own but the glory of God the Father. If you know anything about the moon, you know that the moon gives off no light of its own; it simply reflects the light of the sun. You might say that this is what the Son is to the Father. This is the "radiance" that Hebrews 1:3 is talking about.

The verse also says Christ is the "exact representation" of the Father. The word used here in the original language refers to "a stamp or impress, as on a coin or seal."[1] You've seen the impressions (designs) that are on coins: those impressions are made by a stamp that bears the image it produces. So when you look at a coin, you know exactly what the original stamp looks like. It's the same thing with Christ, the Son. When you look at Him, you can tell what the Father is like.[2]

Jesus—Showing Us How to Image God

When I was in college, I majored in opera. An important way for me to understand opera in its purest form was for my teachers to play videos and audios of the great opera singers. In the same way, God the Father has given us Jesus Christ as a visual example of the image of God. There is no better way to understand the image of God than to look at Jesus Christ. As Anthony Hoekema explains, "What we see and hear in Christ is what God intended for man."[3]

Me: God's Mirror to the World—Heather

Through the example of Jesus, we see how we can become radiant reflectors of God's image. In Luke 2:52, Luke writes that "Jesus grew in wisdom and stature, and in favor with God and men." Consider this verse. Luke is telling us how the young boy, Jesus of Nazareth, developed into the man who became the image of God. From this passage, we see that Jesus reflected the image of God at least four ways: mentally, physically, spiritually, and socially.

Mentally

First, as Luke 2:52 tells us, Jesus grew in "wisdom." Although Jesus was God and, as God, was all-knowing; as a human He grew mentally. As God's image bearers, humans are different from the animals because we have the ability to reason and learn in a way that sets us apart from all of God's other creatures. Commentator Wayne Grudem shares a great illustration of this point: "Beavers still build the same kind of dams they have built for thousands of generations, birds still build the same kind of nests, and bees still build the same kinds of hives. But we continue to develop greater skill in technology and . . . every field of endeavor."[4] In fact, as I write this, I use neither a quill nor a typewriter. I am using a computer. Imagine an ape developing the skill to invent a computer.

Physically

Jesus also grew in "stature"—that is, Jesus grew physically. In a sense, our physical bodies teach us about God's attributes and how we are the image of God. I know what you might be thinking: *how does our physical body play a role in the image of God?* Think about it: our physical bodies give us the ability to see with our eyes. Grudem says,

> This is a Godlike quality because God Himself sees . . . although he does not do it with physical eyes like we have. Our ears give us the ability to hear, and this is a Godlike ability, even though God does not have physical ears. Our mouths give us the ability to speak, reflecting the fact that God is a God who speaks. Our senses of taste and touch and smell give us the ability to understand and enjoy God's creation, reflecting the fact that God himself understands and enjoys His creation.[5]

These physical attributes—our eyes, ears, mouth, etc.—teach us about God's own nature and help us understand how we are like Him.

Spiritually

Jesus also "grew in favor with God." Jesus grew spiritually. His life was "wholly directed toward God."[6] At the beginning of His ministry, though He was tempted by the devil, Jesus obeyed the Father. He often spent entire nights in prayer to the Father, and His prayers were for *God's* will, not His own. He once said, "My food . . . is to do the will of him who sent me and to finish his work"

(John 4:34). At the end of His earthly life, when Jesus was considering the suffering He was about to endure, He prayed, "My Father, if it is possible, may this cup be taken from me. Yet not as I will, but as you will" (Matthew 26:39).

Socially

Finally, Luke 2:52 tells us that Jesus "increased in favor . . . with God and men." In this we see that Jesus grew socially, or relationally. Jesus was completely focused on His neighbor.[7] When people who were in need of healing or food or forgiveness came to Him, He was always available to help them. In John 15:13, Jesus tells us about the greatest love of all: "Greater love has no one that this, that he lay down his life for his friends." This is the kind of love Jesus revealed as the supreme image of God.

Developing the Image of Christ

When I was growing up, the Polaroid was a popular camera. You would take a picture, and it would slowly develop into a clear snapshot. As Christians we are like a Polaroid snapshot. As God through His Spirit works in us, we slowly develop into people who look more like Jesus Christ, the perfect image of God.

What does all of this mean for you? How can you actually begin to look like Jesus? Well, you have to wait till the next chapter. But I will say that it is crucial that we understand how these truths impact our lives, because they are related to our purpose as human beings.

Whose Reflection Do I See?

Opening Scripture: Read Romans 8:29. Ask God to speak to you in a specific way as you study His Word today.

☆ **God's Goal for Your Life:** Has anyone ever asked you to write goals for your life? Maybe a parent or guidance counselor encouraged you to really think about what you wanted to do in the future. Or you may have made yourself write goals for the school year or your summer break. Setting goals helps us stay on the right track and accomplish what we have set out to do. Did you know that God has a goal for your life?

What does the Word say? Reread Romans 8:29. According to this verse, what is God's goal for your life?

- ❑ To witness to my friends
- ❑ To be conformed to the likeness of Jesus
- ❑ To stop sinning
- ❑ To learn to sing

What do you think? Is God's goal for you also your goal for your life? Explain your answer. ______________________________

____

____

While it's OK to have other ambitions for our lives, God's goal for us should be the overarching goal of everything else. You may aspire to

be a veterinarian, doctor, or mom someday in the future, and that is great. But God wants you to be like Jesus as you fill those roles.

Think about it: What are some of the goals that you have for your future? In what ways can you reflect Christ as you meet those goals? ______

____

____

____

☆ **Is It You—or Him?** Take a few minutes to count how many mirrors you look in during the course of an average day. You'll want to count your bathroom mirror, the mirror you keep in your purse, your car mirror, and the one at school. You get the picture. Now let me ask you a question: what if the next time you looked in a mirror you saw someone else looking back at you? You would probably jump a mile in the air. It would be rather strange, don't you think? Well, did you know that when someone looks at you, the reflection they should see isn't you? They should see the reflection of Jesus living in you. Sure they see you—but they should recognize that there is something different about you and the way you live your life. Let's look at four areas of life that God wants to remake into His image.

Fill in the blanks: Read Luke 2:52, and fill in the missing words.

"And Jesus grew in ____________ and __________, and in ________ with ___________ and __________."

1. Mentally. If we are going to be changed into the image of Christ, we need to start with our minds. A wise person once said that what we think determines what we will become. That's why it's so important that we guard the things that we put into our minds.

What does the Word say? Read 2 Corinthians 10:5. What does this passage say that we should do with every thought? ____________________

____

____

What does it mean? What are some practical ways you can take your thoughts captive to Christ? ______________________________

____

____

We are bombarded each day with all kinds of images and ideas that tempt us to lower our standards. The more we fill our minds with the trash of the world, the less our minds will become like Christ.

Think about it: How can you guard your mind against negative influences found on TV, the Internet, and music? ______________________

____

____

2. Physically. Obviously, our bodies are not going to look like Christ, but we can use our bodies in ways that honor Him.

What does the Word say? Read Romans 12:1. In what way can we worship God according to this passage? ______________________

____

____

We can choose to honor God with our bodies or to dishonor Him. The little choices we make such as what we wear, what we eat, and how we act on a date should all reflect Christ.

What's your experience? Is there an action you participate in that does not honor God? If so, what steps can you take to change? ____________

____

____

____

____

3. Spiritually. Just as Jesus spent time alone with His heavenly Father, we must spend time with Him as well. The more time we spend with Him, the more we will find that our desires change to love the things God loves and hate the things He hates.

Fill in the blanks: Read 2 Peter 3:18 and fill in the missing words.

"But ______ in the _________ and ___________ of our Lord and Savior Jesus Christ."

What does it mean? Just as we cannot grow without physical nourishment, we absolutely will not grow unless we have spiritual food. God's Word is that food. The fact that you are taking the time to do this Bible study is a great way for you to grow spiritually. Keep it up, and you'll be amazed at the spiritual muscles He builds in you.

4. Socially. Galatians 5:13 says, "Serve one another in love." The biggest way that we reflect Christ to the world is by loving others with the love of God. The more you become like Christ, the more your life will be characterized by a selfless and loving attitude.

Think about it: In what ways can you practice serving others in love? In your family? Among your friends? How about to those less fortunate than you?

____

____

____

Pray about it: Ask God to help you see others through the same eyes of love that He does. Next, make a list of people whom He has put in your life and called you to love. Pray that you will find tangible ways to serve them this week.

✝ **Living the Word:** Read 2 Corinthians 5:17, 21.

- What does verse 17 teach about who we are if we're Christians?

____

____

____

- Whether or not you feel that it's true, you are a new creation in Christ. Write a short prayer thanking God for making you His new creation. ______________________________

____

____

____

• Because of Jesus's death and resurrection, we can become the righteousness of Christ. How are you cooperating with Him as He remakes you? ____

____

____

____

• Are there some changes you need to make so that you more radiantly reflect Jesus? If so, list them here. Next, share them with a trusted friend or mentor so she can pray with you as you rely on God's power to change. ____

____

____

____

____

____

____

The Christian self-image means understanding that your worth is found in your amazing dignity as God's image bearer.

But we all, with unveiled face, beholding as in a mirror the glory of the Lord, are being transformed into the same image from glory to glory, just as from the Lord, the Spirit.
2 Corinthians 3:18 NASB

Beginning to Look a Lot Like Jesus

Does the name Terri Schiavo sound familiar? She was the woman who, in the spring of 2005, was in the middle of the right-to-die controversy. As I write this last chapter on the image of God, the breaking news is that Terri Schiavo died this morning, March 31, 2005, at the age of forty-one. She died at a hospice in Florida where she had resided for years while her husband and parents fought over her fate in the nation's longest, most bitter right-to-die dispute.[1]

A Distorted Image

How did we get to the point where a segment of our society no longer considers life sacred? How did the ones God created to mirror His image come to reflect such a distorted view?

This tragedy should not surprise us. After all, one of the most popular movies of 2005, *Million Dollar Baby*, promotes the right to die as a good thing.

This film tells the story of Maggie Fitzgerald, a female fighter who becomes a champion in women's boxing. When Maggie suffers a terrible injury in the ring, she is paralyzed from the neck down. And when Maggie is confined to a wheelchair and a body she can't control, she decides she would rather die than accept her limitations. Eventually, her trainer, Frankie Dunn, decides to help Maggie take her own life.

Although the movie was billed as a fight film, it actually promotes the right to suicide. As film critic Michael Medved pointed out to Fox News's Bill O'Reilly, the narrator of the film describes the assisted suicide as "a heroic act to help somebody kill somebody else."[2]

Maggie Fitzgerald decided she did not want to live if living meant she could no longer be a boxing champion. Maggie tells Frankie, "I can't be like this, Boss, not after what I've done. I've seen the world. People chanted my name. I was in magazines."

The world-view of this film is the exact opposite of the Christian's understanding of the value of human life. True Christian love would help Maggie understand that she still possesses human dignity and gifts that could and should be used for the benefit of herself and others.

The Schiavo case reminds us that because of sin the truth about our dignity as humans created in the image of God has been distorted. Legal abortions and right-to-die cases are direct results of our society's failure to understand that humans are intended to reflect the image of God. Sin has steamed up their mirrors. When people misunderstand who they are, they cannot properly reflect God's image to the world. But in Christ the perfect image of God is restored (Colossians 1:15; Hebrews 1:3). And as the verse at the top of this chapter says, when Christians are transformed into the image of Christ, we mirror His glory.

The Practical Side of the Mirror

In the previous chapter, we saw that the image of God involves our whole person, including at least these four aspects: mental, physical, spiritual, and relational. In this chapter, I want to show how these different aspects affect our lives as Christians in practical ways.

Mentally

God has given us minds to *think*—rationally, logically, and creatively. Are you, as the image of God, using your mind as an instrument for the glory of God, or has your mirror become steamed up so that God's glory cannot be seen in you? The Bible says that to grow as a Christian, you must be "renewed in the spirit of your mind" (Ephesians 4:23 NASB). What this means is that in order to guard against being "conformed to this world," you must "be transformed by the renewing of your mind" (Romans 12:2 NASB) through constant time in the Word of God.

So, as I see it, my friend, you have a choice as to how to use your mind when it comes to living in this world. Let's briefly look at just three areas where these choices hit you often.

Entertainment. You can use the mind God gave you to apply godly wisdom when choosing the movies you see, the music you listen to, the Web sites you visit, and the books and magazines you read. Or you can be defined by accepting what pop culture says is OK or cool and hip or "hot." But remember, as you make your choices, you are the image of God.

Education. Since we are talking about the mind, I have to mention school. I know, I know, you think that you get it enough from your parents, but I have to say it. Knowing that your mental abilities serve to image God, use the brain God gave you to do your best in school. I didn't say that you have to make straight As, but you should strive for excellence and work as hard as you can. This is not an option for someone who understands this important call to live as the image of God.

Social judgments. When we see things happening in our culture like what happened to Terri Schiavo, we don't have to listen to what popular culture says about the issue. We should, instead, listen to what the Bible has to say on the matter. And the Bible clearly values *life*!

Physically

Our bodies play an important role in being the image of God. That is why Paul writes, "Glorify God in your body" (1 Corinthians 6:20 NASB). We talked in the last chapter about looking in the mirror and seeing ourselves as the image of God. Because we are in God's image, He wants us to treat our bodies with respect and honor.

Self-worth. I am amazed at how many young people today have a strong sense of self-hate. One day while walking in the mall, I was distressed to see a group of teenagers wearing really dark clothes, all hunched over, with enormous scowls on their faces. It saddened me so much, and I wondered what was going on in their heads. They had this look on their faces that communicated, *I am worthless, and I hate my life.*

But then I realized that I have been guilty of jokingly saying, "I hate myself" when I've done something dumb and am mad at myself. But after I had Ella, I imagined her saying that to herself, and I made myself stop saying it, even in jest. God does not want me to hate myself; He created me in His image. You, too, are created in the image of God. You are of great worth in His sight.

Sexual purity. At our Girls of Grace conferences, we get lots of questions about sex (and we answer many of them in our new book, *Q&A*).[3] When we are sexually impure, we dishonor and disrespect the image of God. Now don't get me wrong. When God created Adam and Eve in His image, He blessed them and told them to "be fruitful and multiply, and fill the earth, and subdue it" (Genesis 1:28 NASB). Did you catch that? As the image of God, men and women are called to reproduce children, who also are the image of God. In other words, sex is instrumental in God's special plan for His creation. God invented sex! But as with so many things, the perversion of a good thing brings all kinds of trouble. And sex has been perverted in all kinds of ways.

There is the "normal" sexual perversion between boys and girls—and by "normal perversion," I mean sex outside of marriage, for this is definitely a perversion of God's plan. And beyond that, there is the perversion of homosexuality. Paul, when describing God's wrath against the sin of humankind, said, "Even the women turned against the natural way to have sex and instead indulged in sex with each other. And the men, instead of having normal sexual relationships with women, burned with lust for each other" (Romans 1:26–27 NLT).

From what Paul says in 1 Corinthians, we see that there's something about sexual sins that sets them apart from other sins: "No other sin so clearly affects the body as this one does. For sexual immorality is a sin against your own body (6:18 NLT). He goes on to explain that one of the things that makes sexual sin different for believers is that our bodies are the home of the Holy Spirit, and our bodies have been bought with a price. When we sin sexually, we violate the Holy Spirit living in us. Paul concludes by saying, "Honor God with your body" (v. 20 NLT).

Sexual purity is not up for debate. Homosexuality and sex outside of marriage are

not included in God's plan for us. They are wrong and sinful and, as a result, very costly.

Cutting. Another question that we've been asked about at every conference is cutting. This is a growing trend among teenagers. If you are one of those girls who cuts herself to feel better inside, I want you to imagine that I am sitting right across from you, holding both your hands in mine, looking straight into your eyes.

Here is what I want to say: "I know that you must be experiencing something very painful inside to want to cause yourself pain, but cutting yourself is not a solution. When you hurt yourself, you are also hurting God. He knows your pain, and He alone is the solution to relieving that pain. If you need forgiveness, He can give it to you. If you need comfort, He can give it to you. If you need direction, He is the Way. And if you need to be saved, He is the last stop. Cling to God, and trust Him with your life. God created your body for His purposes. The only way to overcome your pain is to begin the process of living your life with the full awareness and intention of being God's image bearer physically, mentally, spiritually, and relationally."

Spiritually

God made us as His image bearers, and He has implanted within us a deep capacity to know Him intimately. This intimacy begins with a personal relationship with Jesus Christ.

The relationship begins. Our relationship with Christ begins with a rebirth. John 3:5 says that in order to be a part of God's kingdom, we must be born again by the Spirit of God. As we place our faith in the Lord Jesus Christ, who is the perfect image of God, we are united to Him. We are now "in Christ." So the perfect image that was damaged by our sin begins the process of being renewed through Christ (Colossians 3:10). Our conversion to Christ is made possible by God's amazing grace.

The relationship grows. After we are born into God's family, we have a responsibility to grow in the grace and knowledge of our Lord Jesus Christ (2 Peter 3:18). This means you need to be active in your church, studying and applying your Bible, serving your fellow human beings, and saying no to sinful temptations. In fact, Scripture says we should "flee from youthful lusts and pursue righteousness, faith, love and peace, *with those* who call on the Lord from a pure heart" (2 Timothy 2:22 NASB).

The relationship deepens. We take our relationship with Christ to a deeper level as we create an atmosphere of holiness in our lives. Sounds hard, doesn't it? Living a life of holiness isn't easy. When I invite company to my house, I try to create an atmosphere that will make them feel at home. I make sure my house is clean, a good meal is prepared, and candles are burning that give off a sweet smelling aroma.

In the same way, we need to create an atmosphere in our lives that will make our Lord Jesus Christ at home in our hearts. Don't you realize how short our lives are in light of eternity? Scripture says, "All flesh is like grass, and all its glory like the flower of grass. The grass withers, and the flower falls off " (1 Peter 1:24 NASB). This means that it is foolish to pursue our own agendas. After all, our glory is "like the flower of grass," which dies out every winter. Girls, we need to be pursuing something deeper and more enduring than that. Our purpose is to bring glory to God (Isaiah 43:7). We do this as we grow spiritually and are conformed to the image of Christ (Romans 8:29).

Relationally

God is a relational God. He is the Father, the Son, and the Holy Spirit. These three persons of the Godhead are in perfect communion with one another and make up the one true God. God didn't *need* a relationship with us, but He *wanted* a relationship with us. He created us to be the same way. We need the fellowship of other believers. It is vital in our walk with God. I can even see it already in my six-month-old son, Nate. He is so happy when he is surrounded by his mommy or daddy or even his big sister, Ella. But the minute we walk away, he cries. He already has the need for fellowship. Walking with God requires Christian community. Here's some of what that means for you.

Choose godly friends. Do you have godly friends who will encourage you and hold you accountable? The kind of friends you have is *so* important. You've probably heard the scripture a hundred times, but it's still true: "Bad company corrupts good character" (1 Corinthians 15:33). Who you hang out with really does matter, so choose your friends wisely and with your role as God's mirror in mind.

Treat others kindly. How do you treat others? Both friends and strangers are created in God's image. Furthermore, do you treat people who are different from you or people who annoy you with grace and love? It's not always easy. When I'm driving in my car and someone cuts me off, I can become a different person. I heard someone say one time that when she is behind the wheel, the fruit of the Spirit falls right off her tree.

I'm sometimes guilty of not seeing other people as the image of God. If I did, I would treat them kindly even when they don't treat me right. After all, all persons were created to be the image of God. In fact, Scripture says it is wrong to speak evil of others for the very reason that we are made in the image of God (James 3:9). Girls, wouldn't it remove a lot of stress from your lives if you refused to take part in conversations that are demeaning to others? Treating others kindly in what you say will take you a long way toward mirroring God to others.

Date wisely. If you image God in your relationships, this should play a dominant role in the kind of relationships you build with guys. I've been there, and I know what many of you think: *He is such a nice guy, and he is so cute! I can help him in the spiritual area.* Girls, God never calls us to missionary date. Your relationships play a vital role in imaging God, and so these relationships must be built primarily on a mutual love for God and His Christ. Scripture says, "Do not be bound together with unbelievers; for what partnership have righteousness and lawlessness, or what fellowship has light with darkness?" (2 Corinthians 6:14 NASB).

Becoming God's Image Bearer

A healthy self-image does not mean feeling good about yourself on the basis of your looks, achievements, or behavior. The Christian self-image means looking at yourself in the light of God's work of forgiveness and renewal in your life. It means understanding that your worth is found in your amazing dignity as God's image bearer in all aspects: mentally, spiritually, physically, and relationally.

Look in the mirror and smile; you are a beautiful creation of a creative God. And what do you know—you are beginning to bear a striking resemblance.

STUDY GUIDE

Choosing to Believe the Truth

Opening Scripture: Begin by reading 2 Corinthians 5:21. Ask God to teach you from His Word today.

Rethink Who You Are: If you've turned on the TV lately, you've seen the lineup of makeover shows that are popular with viewers. The show's producers usually pick someone who suffers from low self-esteem and then make her over. They give her new teeth, updated clothes, a cuter nose, and a different body. It's like she was a frog, and now she's a princess. You would think that this girl's whole life would change overnight. But did you know that many times it doesn't turn out that way? The woman who had the makeover may look different on the outside, but she feels the same way on the inside. Why? Because unless we change our thoughts, we'll feel like the same old us. It's the same way with growing in the Christian life. Until we start to believe that what God's Word says is true about us, we'll feel like the same old sinners destined to make the same old mistakes.

What does the Word say? Reread 2 Corinthians 5:21. God made Jesus to become what for us? ______________________________

____

Because of that, what benefit is ours? ______________________________

____

____

____

What's your experience? If you're a Christian, then in Christ you can become the righteousness of God. Have you ever come to a point where you really understood that truth and let it change your life? If so, explain. If not, write a prayer asking God to help you begin to grasp that truth. ____

____

____

____

____

Just as those who have had a makeover, we need to retrain our minds to think about who we truly are. The more we grow in our relationship with Him, the more we act like who He's made us to be.

☆ **The Power of Your Mind:** Your mind truly is the most amazing creation. It has such great power for your good and also for your harm. What you think determines so much of who you become. Have you ever stopped to think about this before? If you constantly think, *I am stupid*, you will never live up to your full potential. If you let your mind believe that, you'll never overcome a habit; you'll live in slavery to that habit for the rest of your life. It's only when we change our negative thinking and replace it with the truth of God's Word that we can break free from the lies that run through our minds.

What does the Word say? Read Romans 8:5–6. Those who have the Spirit of God, meaning Christians, are to set their minds on what? ______

____

____

What is the result? ________________________________

Think about it: Has there ever been a time when you focused your mind on God and His Word and experienced His peace? If so, explain.

____

____

What does it mean? What do you think this verse means by "the mind set on the flesh is death"? ______________________________

____

____

Left to our own direction, or our flesh, our minds can lead us down a dangerous path. That's why it's crucial that we continually renew our minds in God's Word. We can believe anything, whether or not it's true, when we stop running our thoughts through the filter of the Bible. We must constantly guard our minds from the lies that bombard us each day.

Fill in the blanks: Read Philippians 4:6–7 and fill in the missing words.

"Do _______ be anxious about __________, but in ____________, by _____________ and petition, with thanksgiving, present your _____________ to ________. And the ___________ of God, which transcends all understanding, will ________ your _________ and your ________ in Christ Jesus."

Did you see it? There's that word *peace* again. When our minds are yielded to Him, we'll find that most wonderful gift: peace. People would pay millions for it, but money can't buy it. True peace can only be found when we look to God.

☆ **Replace the Lies with Truth:** Maybe you have believed some lies about yourself, and you're tired of living under the weight of those lies. Let's look at three practical steps we can take to replace the lies with truth.

1. Identify the lies. Take some time to think about some of the things you believe about yourself. Maybe you think that you are a dirty sinner who is unworthy of God's love. If so, remember that our opening verse told us that He loved you so much that He died so you could become His righteousness. Maybe you struggle with cutting, like Heather talked about, and you think that the only way to deal with your stress is by hurting yourself. That is a lie! God will help you manage your stress as you rely on Him and His power to change.

Pray about it: Take some time to ask God to show you some of the lies you believe that contradict what He says about you. Write them here.

____

____

____

____

____

2. Pray. Now take your list of lies and bring them to God. Agree with Him that these are not true and that you want to replace them with the truth of His Word. Ask Him to give you verses that contradict the lies that you have believed. The more time you spend talking and listening to Him, the more you will start to recognize His voice of truth speaking into your life.

What does the Word say? Read John 14:6. In what three ways does Jesus describe Himself in this verse? __________________________

____

To overcome the lies, we must continually draw closer to Jesus, who is the Truth.

3. Battle the lies with truth. After we have identified the lies we believe and have prayed about them, then we need to find the ammunition to battle them. Can you guess what our weapon is? You guessed it: the Word of God.

Fill in the blanks: Read Psalm 119:160 and fill in the missing words.

"All your ________ are _______; all _______ righteous ________ are __________."

If you want to battle feelings that you aren't loved, find verses that tell about His unfailing love. If you struggle with thinking you are destined to fail, find verses about God's strength. Then write them out and learn them. Memorize them, and make them a part of your natural thought process. Consider them your mental chewing gum. While you're exercising, think of these verses. While you take a shower, let the truth wash over you. Before long, you will find that the lies you believed have been replaced. Gradually, you will find that it's easier to believe what God says about you.

✔ **Try This:** Look back at the list of lies you are tempted to believe. Now pick one of those lies. Spend some time looking for verses that contradict that lie, and write them in the space provided. You may want to use the concordance in the back of your Bible to help you. Be patient. It may take some time, but as you look, you'll be amazed at how God leads you to just the right verse for your particular struggle. ______________________________

____

____

____

____

____

✝ **Living the Word:** Read Colossians 3:2.

- What do you think this verse means by setting our minds on things above? ____________________

____

____

- What are some earthly things that steal our mind's attention from thinking about the things of God? ____________________

____

____

- What are some practical steps you can take to set your mind on things above? ____________________

____

____

____

____

____

____

Notes

Mouth Management

1. Frank Peretti, *No More Bullies: For Those Who Wound or Are Wounded* (Nashville: W Publishing Group, 2003), 116.

2. Ibid., 150; emphasis in original.

Sanctified Gossip

1. Peretti, *No More Bullies*, 153.

If the Shoe Fits, Wear It!

1. Rick Warren, *The Purpose Driven Life* (Grand Rapids: Zondervan, 2002), 251.

2. Florence Littauer, *Personality Plus: How to Understand Others by Understanding Yourself* (Grand Rapids: Revell, revised 1992).

Dirty Laundry

1. Cynthia Spell Humbert, *Deceived by Shame, Desired by God* (Colorado Springs: NavPress, 2001).

Reflections of a Better Me

1. Wayne Grudem, *Systematic Theology* (Grand Rapids: Zondervan, 1995), 444.

2. Anthony A. Hoekema, *Created in God's Image* (Grand Rapids: Eerdmans, 1986), 72.

3. Ibid., 85.

Jesus—The Mirror Image of God

1. W. E. Vine, "Image," *An Expository Dictionary of New Testament Words* (Old Tappan, N.J.: Revell, 1940; reprint 1966), 247.

2. Hoekema, *God's Image*, 21.

3. Ibid., 22.

4. Grudem, *Systematic Theology*, 446.

5. Ibid., 448.

6. Hoekema, *God's Image*, 74.

7. Ibid.

Beginning to Look a Lot Like Jesus

1. "Terri Schiavo Dies, but Battle Continues," MSNBC news service report, March 31, 2005, http://www.msnbc.msn.com/id/7293186/ (accessed April 12, 2005).

2. Al Mohler, "Million Dollar Baby—Assisted Suicide at the Oscars," http://www.crosswalk.com/news/weblogs/mohler/?adate=2/24/2005#1314506 (accessed April 12, 2005).

3. Point of Grace, *Q&A* (West Monroe, La.: Howard, 2005).

get real with

Bestseller

Girls of Grace Book
ISBN: 1-58229-268-X

ISBN: 1-58229-463-1

Point of Grace, along with Nancy Alcorn, answers questions collected from previous Girls of Grace conferences about family, faith, sex, dating, friendships, themselves, and more.

A thematic collection of ten songs from Point of Grace and some of today's top female Christian artists.

www.wordrecords.com

Girls of Grace Journal
ISBN: 1-58229-440-2

www.howardpublishing.com
Available where good books are sold.

www.pointofgrace.net